The Optimist!

A PATH TO PERSONAL SUCCESS & HAPPINESS

by

Ulf Sandström

The International Bestselling Author of
"Du Blir Vad Du Tänker"
("You Become What You Think")

with Josiah R. Baker, Ph.D.

The Optimist!

Featuring
The Happiest Man in the World

Published by:
Trine Day LLC
PO Box 577
Walterville, OR 97489
1-800-556-2012
www.TrineDay.com
TrineDay@icloud.com

Library of Congress Control Number: 2023933397

Sandstrom, Ulf & Baker, Josiah
–1st ed.
p. cm.

Epub (ISBN-13) 978-1-63424-418-3
Trade Paperback (ISBN-13)978-1-63424-417-6
1. Success. 2. SELF-HELP—Personal Growth—General. 3. SELF-HELP
—Personal Growth—Happiness. 4. SELF-HELP—Personal Growth —
Success. I. Sandstrom, Ulf & Baker, Josiah. II. Title

FIRST EDITION
10 9 8 7 6 5 4 3 2 1

Printed in the USA
Distribution to the Trade by:
Independent Publishers Group (IPG)
814 North Franklin Street
Chicago, Illinois 60610
312.337.0747
www.ipgbook.com

PREQUEL

Identify your.......God, Country, Family, Friends
Know your................Body, Mind, Work, Money
Analyze..Eight Values
Create...Goals
Match.......................................Values with Goals
Repeat..Goals
Feel.......................................Accomplishments

Other Works by Ulf Sandström

You Become What You Think ("Du Blir Vad Du Tänker"), and Yngve Borgström. Forma Publishing Group, 1986, 2000. ISBN: 9789153422051.

You Become What You Dream ("Du Blir Vad Du Drömmer Om"). Forma Publishing Group, 2000. ISBN: 91-534-2206-6.

The Road to Happiness, Sweden Trade Publishing, 2003. ISBN: 0-9744088-0-8.

The Magic Silver Coin, Sweden Trade Publishing, 2006. ISBN: 0-9744088-1-6.

TABLE OF CONTENTS

PART I

INTRODUCTION

Success starts with a positive attitude.

By reading this book, you will embark upon a personal journey of change.

Each day when you awake, you face two choices: *positive, uplifting thoughts*, or *negative, destructive thoughts*. The choice is yours. It is within your power to succeed or fail. You can control your destiny one moment, one hour, and one day at a time.

This book condenses volumes of self-help information into a subtle, powerful message that can renew your sense of purpose and enhance your pursuit of a positive, happy life. Happiness can be forged by a willed desire to learn and improve. Become receptive to positive thinking. Reflect upon its optimistic message and this book will transform your life. Now ... relax ... and enjoy this life-transforming story.

Optimism = Happiness

"How can I improve *my* life?"

A happy life begins with making the right choices, having the right kind of thoughts, and letting them flow freely through your mind. Each day, that choice is yours.

When you awake and embark upon and willfully embrace a positive outlook, that choice will direct your mental orientation for the remainder of that day.

Initiating and developing an optimistic lifestyle requires that you separate yourself from simply reacting to your immediate physical surroundings. Set aside possible knee-jerk reactions, get creative, and change your behavioral patterns!

If you fall into an unhappy state of being, forge a mental path connecting from where you are to where you imagine being.

Mental discipline enables you to act more independently exert your free will. This will liberate you from negative, destructive thinking.

So, how can you liberate yourself? How can you improve your life?

First, identify and prioritize your goals from your dreams. Be honest with your true desires. Once you clearly comprehend your goals, you can reach for them by using the powers inherent in your incredible, subconscious mind.

Like any tool, your mind can be willfully applied in ways that can yield fruitful results. Purposely training yourself to use the powers you have, that are locked up in your subconscious mind, will give you more control and power over your thoughts and actions. By thinking both positively and repetitively, you can be liberated from seemingly insurmountable circumstances, by thinking in a new way. Importantly, you will get positive, life-changing results.

For many years, humanity has sought ways to uncover the secrets of fulfilling life's wants and desires. In this book, we will stress that persistence and a positive attitude will open the path that will lead to a balanced, happy, and prosperous life.

Be patient and, with repeated optimistic efforts, you can transform your life. The path you want to follow is not formed by accident. It is formed by setting goals and establishing priorities. Each goal should have sub-priorities. Do you want to lead a successful life? Use your imagination to motivate your efforts. Become excited by the thought of completing your goals. Consider how you can link all possible actions to fulfill your present goals. When listing your top priorities, choose those that will harmoniously give you balance and success.

Define what is most important in your life.

It's not selfish to think about what's most important to you in your life. Almost all personal goals fall within the scope of the eight values presented in this book. Take a few moments to consider what is most important in your life. Then write it down. We have provided places for you to write notes throughout this book. As you learn more, and write more, your notes will reflect your progress.

Your First Exercise

For this first exercise, write a short list of what makes you happy, and briefly explore ways you might use to meet these goals.

Your Lists

Personal goals are as limitless as your own imagination. Some goals are easily defined and can clearly be accomplished, such as finding a better or higher paying job. Other goals are complicated and may require many steps and procedures, such as nurturing harmonious relationships. Sort your basic goals from those that are more complicated. As you organize your efforts, your priorities will emerge and your focus will improve, as you strive to fulfill your goals. It is that simple.

The Key

Successfully making your dreams come true is achieved by creating the right state of mind: you must trust your innermost mind, which has the power to transform your dreams into reality. This is best done by developing positive mental habits that enable you and your efforts to succeed.

Usually, your first obstacle is how to handle your sub-conscious mind, a subtle and self-serving part of your brain which controls much of your decision-making and, more importantly, your habits.

For many people, their subconscious mind holds them back because it has accepted and learned negative thinking habits. Sometimes, of course, other people and life events can intrude and negatively influence or re-enforce destructive thinking. These thoughts may arise in self-defense, but if they dominate your life after a crisis is over, they must be eliminated

To make best use of your sub-conscious mind, you must transform your negative habits into positive ones within your subconscious mind by thinking: "I will achieve my goal." Push aside your negative thoughts. Focus on repeating goal-related, positive thoughts. By doing so, you'll initiate your first steps to forging a new optimistic reality that will lead to a better life.

As you will see, very soon, subtle wonders will happen that will transform you from within, affecting your mind, spirit, and attitude. Embracing the positive will change your life. We are certain of that. Over the years, we have witnessed many people achieve success by applying this simple principle.

Ideas = Reality

Napoleon Hill once said, "thoughts are things," meaning that your subconscious mind sends and receives signals which then ascend to your conscious mind and your body.

From you, they are then broadcast to the world around you. Ideas behave like radio signals.

For almost all of us, being alive at this point in human history is a good reason to feel happy. Technological, social, political, and commercial freedoms and inventions have liberated us from many of the countless physical burdens of the past. Consider all the great conveniences and liberties surrounding you. Carefully contemplate your many skills and talents. Be grateful and appreciate what you have already achieved.

Recognizing your true greatness and potential will boost your ability to feel success. It will help you embrace increased happiness. Because of how your subconscious and conscious mind work together, the consequences of good choices create happiness and feelings of success as your mind unifies its thoughts. Yes, you can change what may be perceived as "fate" by positively steering your ship of life toward your dreams' most desirable destinations.

This Story – and Your Story

As you continue to read this book, think of eight things in your life that you are thankful for, and as you do, write them down. See the space for you to write them, below:

_____

_____

_____

_____

_____

Writing down these positive thoughts helps your subconscious mind to focus on those parts of your life that boost your happiness.

Reflecting upon the positive amplifies your confidence in fulfilling your planned goals, so it may be important to ignore any intruding, non-critical short-term problems. Most answers to short-term problems will gradually emerge within your mind is ready. Don't allow small obstacles or distractions to obscure your mind's focus on the positive.

As children, we don't learn these principles at school. It may also surprise you to learn that such secrets of success are rarely taught in many homes, so, let's get going!

Our time is precious. We only temporarily live on this beautiful planet, so we must make the most of our lives. Dedicating yourself to aim for your best possible future is an integral part of fulfilling your dreams.

Continual daily efforts, as you embark upon this journey, will lead you along a lifetime path of more fulfillment and more happiness. As you read, remain relaxed. Reflect upon your innermost thoughts ... and ask yourself:

Who am I?

What do I represent?

How can I better myself?

How can I improve my relationship with others?

How can I make a difference in the world?

Often people go through life reacting to situations with pre-existing mental habits which may have been created on a very primitive level for mere survival. Many of us unwittingly suffer from old negative, self-protecting prejudices and biases that exist and permeate our present thinking. Shrug off your old, negative reactionary ways. Do it by identifying and creating new possibilities.

Remember, people who only react to what is presented to them often lack the focus and will to change or improve their lives. Their awareness is limited by their own self-imposed tunnel-vision. People risk becoming cognitively fixated – literally stuck in a rut – by allowing their automatic reactions that likely were learned when they were relatively helpless, to rule their present lives. These are people who will never know what they truly want in life because their conscious and subconscious minds are distracted and off course, ruled by fear and *their automatic reactions.*

People who only react are captains of a ship that is adrift at sea, uncertain of which port they will encounter next. In life, when you visualize and establish your goals, you can break free from reactionary thinking by following the proactionary path taught in this book.

These fundamental questions help you define and enhance your ability to discover a greater meaning in your life. Such questions enable you to identify what's important to you, to obtain balance and enduring happiness.

This book identifies eight "magic" values that will deepen your appreciation and give you a vision of the purpose of life itself. These values are based on universal principles that are already implanted within you. Happiness is obtained by setting goals for you to recognize within each value.

Often people go through life by reacting to situations with pre-existing mental habits which may have been created on a very primitive level for mere survival. Many of us unwittingly suffer from old negative, self-protecting prejudices and biases that exist and permeate our present thinking. Shrug off your old, negative reactionary ways. Do it by identifying and creating new possibilities.

Do not let short-term distractions cause you to aimlessly drift in an open sea of confusion and frustration. Mentally creating and projecting trusted goals is a key component to liberating your life from negative and destructive habits. Remind yourself often of your goals, after you create them. Identify what is truly important to you. Imagine ways to reach your planned destinations. Sketch out your steps so you can visualize becoming the person you want to be. Developing such focus power enhances your ability to control your destiny. As your inner confidence grows, so will your feelings of accomplishment and peace of mind.

When It Seems Impossible...

At times, life can present "unsolvable" problems. Because life and resources are limited, we cannot solve everything all the time. However, sometimes these "unsolvable" problems can eclipse our hopes or distract us from addressing solvable problems. Change what you can, when you have the ability to do so. Then prioritize your efforts using your existing talents and resources.

Positive optimistic thoughts (such as loving, serving, believing, hoping, creating, and enjoying) when they come to dominate your conscious mind, will then unfold miracles in your life. As you continue on this course, your subconscious mind that never sleeps, and controls most of your actions, will begin to generate re-affirming thoughts. If you act upon these positive, inspirational thoughts that seem to come from nowhere, you will start reaching your goals. You will get to your chosen destination.

To obtain success, remember that you first must start by writing down your goals. Second, reflect and visualize your written goals so that they become real in your mind. Last, with repetition and persistence, you can change patterns in your subconscious mind. Your subconscious mind's new positive messages, which you will teach it, will then help you to fulfill your new dreams, just as Woody and Carl achieved them in this book's novella.

Remember, your subconscious mind is primitive. It's primal. It seeks to live forever and cannot distinguish the true differences between reality and fantasy, so you can immediately start feeding it positive, goal-oriented thoughts. Nurture your positive ideas when they form in your head, because this is evidence that your subconscious mind is trying to instruct your conscious mind.

Let it do so, and gradually, your subconscious mind will reach the stage that it will more consistently feed you positive thoughts, which will make you feel better. When those feelings and positive thoughts arrive, keep repeating them as they propel you toward obtaining your goals and accomplishments.

Become truly dedicated! Dedicate yourself to positive goals by developing the virtuous, repetitious, self-affirming thoughts that your subconscious mind will begin to feed to you each day, if you do your homework. Your subconscious mind knows how to navigate your life down many ancient pathways to success and survival. You inherited your subconscious mind's survival skills from true winners, who lived long enough to successfully create the next generation.

This marvelous principle works also for short-term situations. For example, when real danger confronts you, your subconscious mind's earlier programming can miraculously help you escape life-threatening situations. It should comfort you to realize that your subconscious mind can be used as a tool of achievement, rather than as a source of stress, concerns and negativity.

What a great feeling!

About This Book's Novella

This book's novella ("The Happiest Man in the World"), or mini-novel, is embedded with many truths. Internalize its messages, for they can dramatically improve your life.

Embrace the miracle of life itself, which is something amazing that you experience every moment. Realizing this novella's full message takes time: some people may read the story two or three times. Remember, you are extremely lucky to be here in this wonderful world.

Why You Are Extremely Lucky

Your luck began before you were born. In the race for your conception, you beat several million competitors as your sperm fought its way to find that one released egg among hundreds of eggs that remained unavailable. You then survived the pregnancy and the birth. Your very existence is a miracle! Always remember that you are fortunate to be alive ... despite what challenges you might face, you beat the odds from the very beginning. All of us have won the lottery!

Decide to create an optimistic path for yourself. **Today you can change your life!** Repeat it in the morning, during the day, and right before you fall asleep at night: **"tomorrow will be the best day of my life."**

Believe it, and you will see how your life can change!

The greatest secret of our lives is that when we set our mind to accomplish something bigger than ourselves. Our fantastic, incredible sub-conscious mind will take us there. Just let it! When you, as an individual, use your sub-conscious mind, you can transform ideas into reality. Successful inventions and innovations are created by forward, optimistic endeavors. We are born winners – and we continue to be winners each and every day. Remind yourself that you are an optimistic individual.

Choose optimism today ... and success will follow!

Being born winners, we remain winners no matter what we encounter in life. No matter how low we personally sink, we can always improve our situation.

You're not a loser unless you give up. The great spirit of determination and persistence will lift you to higher ground. By focusing on your passionate beliefs, you can reignite your pursuit of happiness, a fundamental human right listed in the United States' Declaration of Independence.

"What is happiness?" you may ask. "How can I increase my happiness? How can I find a fulfilling life?"

Treat this book as your personal manual. Have it accompany you in your pursuit for a brighter future. Its message will nurture you as you work toward success. Its concepts are purposely concise, so you can readily refer to them and apply them in your daily living. Today. Tomorrow.

What is about to be revealed is known to some but practiced by few. Therefore, read this book often. Why is repetition important? This is how learning occurs!

Its most important message: break free from your old habits! Rid yourself of those familiar negative thoughts that pester or distract you from success. You can do it! We know you can!

Part II "**The Optimist**," is a story that presents positive thinking strategies. Become involved with its message. Place yourself into the characters of Carl and Woody, or a mixture of both. Visualize yourself in their roles and imagine yourself in this story. Consider why Carl and Woody experience problems. How did they overcome their obstacles and obtain *success*?

Part III defines your **Eight Values** and **Eight Magic Words,** which will show you how to enhance every facet of your life, while eliminating your fears. In the beginning, new thought processes are difficult to create and keep because we must change our thought habits – but create and keep them anyway. Your potential reward is enormous: you can become a different and better person.

Part IV summarizes the pursuit of happiness, so you can apply these principles in your life and for those that you love. As you become stronger, you'll become better-prepared to help others along the path. This journey towards happiness will be revealed by introducing a scientifically proven technique that will transform your dreams and goals into reality.

Once you develop your own pattern of success, share what you have learned with the world. Teach others how to transform themselves into more optimistic, positive people. Show the people you love how to focus on worthy goals, worthwhile to achieve. As you teach them, your own success will grow! Now relax and start reading...!

PART II

THE HAPPIEST MAN IN THE WORLD

My name is Carl. I have an incredible life-changing story to tell. My life didn't start off so great, but it became quite remarkable.

I had just turned thirty years-old and lived alone in a small, low-rent, sparsely furnished apartment. As so many before me, I attended college, but didn't finish. I then spent most of my twenties working one short-term job after the other, uncertain of myself and what I wanted to become. I was drifting and lost a couple of girlfriends because of it.

Until recent months, I always had roommates, but when the last one left without warning. I was stuck paying the entire rent, which absorbed the small amount of savings that I had cobbled together. To make matters worse, my boss just let me go from my job for showing: "lack of enthusiasm."

My aging car was always breaking down. I ate unehalthy food and rarely exercised. I would languish on my couch mindlessly watching basketball and hockey games for hours. Life felt pointless. I wasn't sure what to do with myself. I had no concrete goals. I lacked any vision of a future. Realizing I had very little money left, one evening, I decided to go for a long walk rather than burn up gas in my old, dying car. However, it was on that one, gorgeous evening that my life forever changed...

Walking along Tampa's scenic Bayshore Boulevard, I kept looking at the slowly setting sun over the beautiful Florida sub-tropical bay. I still didn't know what I wanted to do with my life, except I knew I needed help ... and guidance. I stopped. Closed my eyes, and silently pleaded for help.

Moments later, as I gazed up at the emerging twilight sky, I saw a bald eagle. Right behind the soaring, glorious bird was a glowing star.

"What a beautiful sight!" I thought.

Just then, the eagle began flying towards me – I didn't know what to think!

As it rapidly descended right at me, I temporarily panicked, but just when the bird appeared to seemingly attack, it simply released a gold coin which fell and rolled at my feet. The splendid bird then vanished into the purple sky. It was hard to imagine that something so crazy had just happened, but there was the coin, lying there, on the ground!

Gazing at this shiny coin, I admired its brilliance. But was it real? What would happen if I touched it? Slowly, I reached for it and felt its cool surface in my hand. Then, an inexplicable, incredible burst of happiness radiated within me. As it increased, I became puzzled, confused, and astonished.

Suddenly, a deep and powerful voice from the sky called out, ***"You ... have ... a choice."***

Stunned, I couldn't speak. "Choice?" I thought. "What do you mean by 'choice'?"

"The coin has eight life values," the Voice continued. *"Pick money as one value, or pick the other seven values."*

My hands shook as I saw the coin's inscribed values.

"Here is the secret to finding happiness," the Voice explained, with its sound and presence overwhelming my senses.

I still couldn't speak: I could only gaze, stupefied, at this alluring, brilliant coin.

*"Your choice is simple, Carl. There are four 'relationship' values: **God, country, family, and friends.** There are four 'individual' values: **body, mind, work, and money.** If you choose money, it will cost you the other values, but you will*

gain wealth beyond what you can imagine. Now ... you must make a choice."

Time came to a halt.

The temptation to pick the money value grew as I began believing how it would solve all my problems.

Billions of dollars. Trillions of dollars, even. I imagined how money would change my life. I then wondered, "What about the other values?"

I knew my time to choose was nearly expired when my heart made a distinct, firm decision. "Forget about the money!" I blurted out. "I pick the other seven values!"

"Many chose money, but you did not. You have faith in yourself. Now, you will find success, but without money. Even so, true success will only happen if you fulfill a promise to Me."

"What promise?" I reflected.

"You will meet a wealthy, miserable man. He will ask why you are so happy, despite having no money.

You must embark on a journey across America for eight days with him, each day showing a reflection of one of the eight values. You must explain to him how you found happiness with each value. Plan this journey carefully."

"How will I find happiness?"

*"The secrets of happiness will soon be revealed. For now, the coin will be your own companion, reminding you of the eight values of life. Each day, focus on the two slogan words. **Love** and **serve** on one side. **Create** and **enjoy** on the other."*

"Love, serve, create, enjoy," I mumbled.

I then asked, "Why are you giving me this mission? Who are you?"

"The gold coin will remind you," the Voice repeated, ignoring my questions. *"Carry the coin. Learn its eight values. Study the eight values each day. Let it sink inside you. Apply the slogans with each value. Ardently believe in your thoughts. Create new slogan sentences to apply to your life. Do this each day. Make it a regular habit, like eating.*

Do it four times a day: when you arise, twice when you take time to be alone, and before you go to sleep. Over time, by following this regimen, you will realize tremendous, positive changes. You will find happiness and success."

"But, I don't want to live in poverty."

"Fulfill your promise and that, too, will be added unto you, and you will find what you seek."

Suddenly, the glowing star in the sky brightened. As my eyes became transfixed on its magnificent sight, a feeling of extreme peace overwhelmed my mind as the Voice continued to speak.

"You now will begin your journey towards happiness. Remember, never give up! Visualize your future goals. See them as if they are real, and they will become reality."

As the sunset faded into night, I still stood where I was, clinging to the coin ... transfixed with awe and amazement.

The full moon arose, shining brilliantly in the darkened sky.

19

The Divine Presence diminished as I stood, transfixed, unwilling to even move while I could still feel it.

Then, it disappeared. Overwhelmed and exhausted, I wanted to sit at a nearby park bench, but I never made it. My feet had no feeling in them: suddenly, I collapsed as I blacked out.

When I awoke, it seemed like I lived in another year or in another place, in some kind of vast, expanding world. Amazingly, my mind and body felt tremendously renewed and refreshed. I was temporarily unsure of where I was, but then I noticed that the moon was still shining and was reflecting against Tampa Bay's calm, glittering waters. At first, I wondered if I had lived through some kind of intense hallucination, or strange dream, but then I reached into my pocket, and felt something ... when my hand pulled out the gold coin with its unique inscriptions, I knew it wasn't my imagination.

A jubilant feeling overcame me.

Holding the coin in my hand, I asked, "What must I do next? What does this mean?" And would I remember everything I was supposed to do?

From that evening onward, I kept my promise to the Divine Voice a secret, even though my life began to positively change in many ways ... except for earning money.

Yet, each day I repeated the eight values and my slogans four times. I even wrote them down from time to time. I became focused on how I could improve myself in all of these values, just as the Divine Voice instructed me to do.

"Each day, I repeated the eight values and my slogans four times. I even wrote them down."

Write your thoughts here:

_____

_____

_____

_____

_____

_____

Within a few months, amazing events began happening. Certain "accidents" began happening in my life that I ascribed to the Hand of God. It began when I met a gorgeous, wonderful girl. We fell in love and absolutely adored each other. We had so much fun and so much in common. We could talk and laugh about anything. We soon married. Within a few years, we had two wonderful children. We adored them and gave them lots of love.

My work became much more meaningful.

The customers at Joe's Café appreciated me for my friendliness and the great service I gave them. I was very popular among my co-workers because I created a fun, stimulating atmosphere at the café.

The Divine Voice was right. My life was transformed. I felt close to God. I volunteered in community projects. I had a loving family, and great devoted friends. Every day felt like a miracle. Thank you, thank you, Divine Voice!

The Miserable Billionaire

Eventually, thanks to the Divine Voice's message, I became the general manager of one of Tampa's most successful cafes.

Though I worked many hours, I always was service-oriented and tried my best to make our customers feel welcome. Sometimes hundreds of people would come and go, depending on the day and the season. My workdays continued to be long, but they enabled me to earn enough to support most of my family's needs.

Of all the people that would come and go, there was one man who stood out.

Often, this man strolled over from a nearby office building, accompanied by two or three bored-looking assistants. He almost always barked out orders on his cell phone while he bought stacks of pastries and several rounds of different coffees. As he consumed the pastries, he would continue to talk on the phone, his face often flushed a deep red, as if he were about to explode. Some of my staff dreaded serving him. Rumors circulated that he was an eccentric former politician. The hefty man often would stumble out of his limousine and claim his "spot" (a table beside a fountain, with a splendid view overlooking the Bay), even if somebody already sat there.

When drunk, the middle-aged man sometimes slapped down enormous cash tips on the table, which partly compensated for his rude behavior. We continued to serve him as we would anyone else, but over time it grew increasingly difficult, especially because the man acted as if he owned the place.

Eventually, his behavior worsened.

He more frequently threw himself down at "his" table, drunk, and would obnoxiously yell insults at other customers.

Clearly, he was unhappy and miserable, but with his "servants" always close by, doing whatever he demanded, he always got what he wanted. Or so it seemed.

One day towards the end of my shift, the man approached me with a scowled face. For once, he was alone. As he came closer, I smelled Scotch on his breath. His three-piece suit reeked of an odd mixture of cigarettes and cigars. As usual, he was unshaven. His eyes were bloodshot. His hands and feet trembled slightly as he struggled walking towards his "spot."

Glaring at me, he clumsily motioned towards me. When I reached his table, he snapped, "Give me some coffee. I need caffeine. Got a big deal tonight."

Immediately, I served him of a large pot of coffee and his usual – a dozen assorted pastries.

The man immediately pushed the plate of desserts away and shouted, "Can't you see that I'm alone?! How the hell am I gonna eat all of this crap? And damn, I need this much sugar like a hole in my head!"

Instantly, I removed half of the items.

A few minutes later, I returned. I knew better than to say a word, so I simply waited for him to speak.

The man seemed to be in a state of crisis which impelled me to linger near his table. As I stood there, the man stared at me, as if studying every feature of my body. Just as I nearly left to serve other customers, he yelled, "Your name's Carl, isn't it?"

He then continued, in a tense voice. "Everyone says that you're such a great guy. Such a nice guy. I've seen your pretty wife. Somehow, you guys are just so happy. With no money! And I just broke up with my third bimbo girlfriend this year! What the hell? What makes you so special? And why do so many people like you?"

"How do you know that so many people like me?" I asked, while I calmly collected some of the items off his table.

"Hey! Sit down here!" he suddenly snapped, still acting somewhat drunk despite downing two cups of coffee.

Reluctantly, I sat across from him, uncertain of what he wanted.

Extending a slightly trembling hand, he uttered, "Lots of people call me 'Boss.' But you can call me 'Woody'!"

He then pointed at a cluster of nearby buildings and grumbled. "You might've heard people calling me other names. After all, I own pretty much everything around here, including the building holding this fairly profitable cafe."

I then recalled having heard the café owner complain about the building's owner being a jerk – yet now I stared directly at him.

"So, I kind of 'work' around here," Woody chuckled. "And, I've noticed how great you are with people."

Drinking a big gulp of coffee, Woody went on, "I've seen how you spread happiness around your customers and co-workers. So, I'd like to offer you a position working as one of my personal butlers. You'll work directly for me, instead of languishing here at this dump, with no future."

Hearing his harsh words made me feel a little insulted. I had worked longer at the café than anywhere in my life. It had brought me much needed stability and countless hours of good times. But, then I considered, "Is this the Divine Voice, leading me to another opportunity?"

Noticing me contemplating offer inside my mind, Woody proceeded, "Tomorrow afternoon. Around three. Bring your family over to my house."

"Sure," I found myself responding. Despite some uncertainty of what this man really wanted from me, I accepted, believing that the Divine Voice sent me this opportunity.

"Go look me up," Woody practically insisted, handing me his business card. He then added, sarcastically, "People say 'wonderful' things about me on the internet!"

Before getting up, he grumbled, "And, don't worry about your boss, Frank. He'll easily find someone else to manage this place."

That evening, when I got home, I told my wife of the news. Instead of acting concerned, she responded very positively. She was even excited to go with the children to visit the house of the owner of the company I worked for.

Next Day, 2:15pm

We were surprised when a black stretch limousine stopped at our apartment. Woody's chauffeur patiently waited while we prepared to go. My wife, as she led our kids into the limousine, asked him, "Why did he send you over?"

"I never ask why the boss orders anything, Ma'am," the silver-haired slender man flatly replied. "I just do as I am told."

Although taking my first limousine ride made me feel a bit anxious, my wife and children were excited. Soon, we entered the Bay Area's wealthiest neighborhood, and shortly after that, we turned onto a lane where several armed guards waited at the gate of Woody's incredible, sprawling estate. After they waved us through, the chauffeur drove us along the estate's park-like gardens until we eventually reached a palatial mansion overlooking beautiful Tampa Bay. There, we turned onto a long, circular driveway. When the limousine stopped under an ivy-covered carriage entrance, we were let out and led up a flight of marble stairs, where Woody, dressed in a nice suit, met us at the top.

"These stairs were carved right out of Italian mountains," Woody mumbled under his breath, as his staff assembled around at the double-doorway. With a sigh, he sarcastically added, "Welcome to my little abode."

After Woody rattled off the names of his attending staff members, he pushed me forward and ordered his head butler, "Take the wife and kids into the informal receiving parlor. Take good care of them."

Glancing back at my wife, I expected her to act nervous, but again she appeared excited. Our children, with a look of amazement and wonderment in their eyes, acted as if they had just entered an enchanted castle.

Determined to discuss business, Woody then led me through a pair of carved mahogany doors and down a lengthy vaulted hall filled with portraits and fine art. Eventually, we reached his private sitting-room, adjacent to his personal office.

In awe, I gazed at the ornate furniture, which included a harpsichord, and a collection of antiquities from around the world. Having never seen such a place, I marveled, "This is like a museum."

For the first time, Woody cracked a laugh. "Yeah, that's what my second wife said when she first came here. Good thing I had her sign a solid pre-nup. Got rid of her within a year."

I didn't know how to respond to that.

"Sometime, ha! I'll tell you the whole story over a fine bottle of Scotch," Woody boasted, grinning. He added, "You do like Scotch, don't you?"

Before I could answer, he offered me a chair. Just as I sat down, he handed me a stack of papers with lists on them.

"Since I'm a very, very busy man, I need your help handling my ongoing flow of guests. You'll coordinate events with my personal assistant. You two will work a lot together. She's alright. Very patient. Hell, she puts up with me!"

I nodded, gazing at the paperwork consisting of lists of tasks and social events that needed to be organized.

"And by the way," Woody gruffly added, "your wife will like her, too. She has nothing to worry about because she's not so pretty."

Giving out a slight laugh, he then automatically presented two glasses and poured our drinks. Sliding my double Scotch forward, he asked, "So, what do you think? You leaving that dump of a café and working here?"

"It's quite a long drive from where I live," I mused, out loud.

"Oh, I forgot," Woody replied. "I'll send movers over and pack up your place. You guys can live in one of my bigger cottages in the back."

"A cottage?"

"Well, it's got four bedrooms. That oughtta fit your family," Woody noted. "You'll pay no rent. No utilities. No commute. And I will match your old salary at the café."

He scribbled down a number on a notepad, demonstrating that he already knew what I earned.

"For a while, I've considered how you might work here," Woody confessed, with a glum tone. "See, my staff is unhappy and you've got this infectious happiness about you. We need that kind of presence here."

Inside, while I struggled containing the thrill of having such a fortuitous opportunity, Woody then hastily added, "C'mon! Say 'yes'. To sweeten the pot, I'll pay you ten percent more."

Feeling like I was jumping off a high diving board, I agreed, "Okay!"

My first few months working for Woody were unusual in that I almost never saw him. He was always busy in meetings, often away on trips, or he would arrive home very late and very drunk. Though my wife and children were happy living on the gorgeous estate, I began questioning my decision to change jobs. It was an odd feeling because my work was much easier than at the café. Living rent-free on the estate for the first time in our marriage, we could actually start saving some money. Less work, easier work, and more money – so why was I not feeling fulfilled?

Almost all of Woody's staff had worked for him for many years. They were the ones who had learned how to put up with his bad temper and could tolerate his rudeness and thoughtlessness. I soon realized that Woody was a very secretive man who avoided meeting new people. Hence, he kept his staff intact, with few changes. But the staff hardly knew him. Even his personal assistant, Rachel, rarely had conversations with him of any substance. It became clear to me that Woody was indeed a very lonely man.

The fancy portraits in the mansion's hallways were acquired by auction: Woody didn't display any family photos. As the weeks passed, I never heard him ever mention his family. His birthday came and went without anybody saying a word.

In fact, he had ordered Rachel to make sure that nobody wished him a "Happy Birthday." Woody disappeared for most of that week. I later learned that he frequently went to Las Vegas, but he always came back alone – still unhappy, stressed, and miserable.

I finally asked him, after his third or fourth trip there, "Woody, what do you do in Vegas?"

His reply was simple, "What goes on in Vegas ... stays in Vegas."

He then marched into his private office, shut the door, and I didn't see him for a couple of days.

Rachel, his personal assistant spent a good portion of her time teaching me how to reorganize Woody's old business files. Much of it was from the numerous companies that he had acquired. Being a meticulous, detailed-oriented person, he demanded everything to be perfectly recorded, controlled, and organized. Though I had no previous training in accounting or bookkeeping, I quickly learned.

I eventually discovered that Woody had a talent for buying internet companies at a very low price and then got them into special niches where they would earn large profits. His fortune was also rapidly growing in real estate. Though he never explained the original source of his wealth, Woody was obviously accustomed to always having plenty of money.

And that was the catch: although Woody was extremely financially successful, I soon noticed that he had no relationship with God, his country, his community, family or friends.

What is your relationship with God, Country, Community and Family? (Write it down here)

_____

_____

_____

_____

_____

_____

Those four principles that anchored my life and gave it purpose were almost unknown to Woody. Woody's whole life revolved around earning even more money and amassing even more wealth. But for what? He neglected everything else important in life. It was becoming obvious to me that his life was negative in every area except money – the opposite of my situation. In fact, I overheard Woody on many occasions complain about how he hated his work … and his life.

It took a while longer than I had initially expected, but after working six months at the estate, I became good friends with the entire staff. My life went well despite the unexpected change in daily responsibilities at Woody's mansion, so different from the café work that I loved. But I still looked at the coin and meditated four times a day, and diligently continued to practice what the Divine Voice told me.

A Thanksgiving Crisis

With our new situation, Thanksgiving Day had turned into a big event for us. My wife, feeling very happy with her new beautiful, larger kitchen on the estate, decided to host a Thanksgiving dinner for many of our friends and some of Woody's staff.

That afternoon, everyone was having a great time enjoying each other's company and eating the delicious food. Our children were playing games and our friends were appreciating the cozy, friendly atmosphere in our guest house.

We all were enjoying our time together, giving thanks to God for everything we had, grateful for living in a free, largely peaceful country. We thanked all the brave Americans in the armed services, who protected our freedom.

While we were enjoying our friendly and relaxing get-together, the front door suddenly swung open ... and standing there was Woody. He was intoxicated, with a disheveled appearance. Clearly miserable and unhappy, his face flushed red, Woody could hardly stand on his feet.

"I was putting in extra hours into this acquisition..." he mumbled under his breath, staring at us all. "And began wondering... why the hell did everybody ask for the day off...?"

My wife gave me a puzzled look. Having spent very little time with Woody, she didn't realize how socially isolated he was. In her own sweet, generous way, she simply pointed at our carved turkey and food on the table, and said, "We're having Thanksgiving ... and you are welcome to join us."

"Ohhh," Woody muttered, a bit embarrassed. Amazingly, he hadn't realized what day it was. I still could not tell which he was: more drunk, or more exhausted. He was so often both.

"I suppose I interrupted your dinner," he stated. He paused, and I could see his eyes blink a couple times. "Hmm. So it is Thanksgiving Day, is it? Hmm ... Oh well."

"Would you like something to eat?" my wife offered, trying to be kind.

Woody pointed at the freshly made cranberry sauce. "You got any chilled vodka I could mix that with?"

My wife didn't know how to react. I said, "Let's get some fresh air, Woody," as I led him gently outside. There we stood together, at our front door. When he said nothing, I asked him, "Are you okay?"

"Why wouldn't I be okay?! Woody defensively blurted out, his red face momentarily reflecting anger. "I'm rich!"

I waited in silence, until he got control of himself.

Finally, he mumbled, "I prefer to avoid Thanksgiving. Let the world observe its silly holidays. It's all a waste of my time!"

Seeing my gesture of helplessness in the face of such disregard for our basic traditions, he added, "Well, I guess I've been under more stress than usual. Stock holders. Transaction deals to worry about. I lost track of what day it was."

"Black Friday's coming up," I replied. "So, do you need me today?"

Woody grew slightly nervous and uttered, "Carl, I came here to talk to you about something else. Fact is, I can't help notice how easily you have made so many friends. You know, I deal with people every day. People that I don't trust. But then there are guys like you. I trust you. It's a gut thing."

Looking at me intensely, he added, "Not everybody can be so incredibly happy all the time like you. And here you are so healthy. So positive about life. You even love your work. Yet, you have practically no money. ***How can you be so happy without money?!***"

At that moment, I knew the Divine Voice had led him to me – Woody was the person I was supposed to show the way to happiness!

Having prepared myself for that moment, I said, "It will take sixteen days, but if you can give me that much time, I can show you how to live a balanced and happy life."

"Sixteen days? Hmm," Woody mumbled, weighing out my proposal.

"We need to take a trip for sixteen days, to eight different places. At each destination, we will talk about how to find happiness."

Woody's eyes shifted towards me. I saw despair, but also sparks of interest.

"I don't know, Carl. Sixteen days away from my work…!"

I waited, as he mulled over the idea. Finally, Woody's big hand reached for mine. It was a rare gesture of trust.

"Okay," he said. "I'm in. Show me the destinations. I'll have my personal assistant work out a schedule to fit it in with my calendar."

"It will change your life," I promised.

"To be honest with you," he confessed, "I am more than unhappy. I'm wretched! Years ago, I thought I'd be happy if I had a billion dollars. But I'm still miserable. Now, I feel worse than I ever have. As you can see, I have no personal life. I've never had a relationship with a woman last longer than a year or so. I've had three failed marriages, plus, there's a teenage son that I hardly know."

"You have a son?"

"Yes, he's gone off to a fine school in England. He only calls when he needs money. And here, you have all this faith in humanity. All this faith in God. I've watched you. But me? I have no religion." Woody sighed. "I'm not connected to this community. Hell, I'm from New Jersey! I live in Florida mainly to avoid taxes!"

Sighing again, he confessed, "My health ... it isn't so good. I eat too much. Drink too much. I'm plagued by swarms of ugly thoughts. The only thing I love is my money ... but I don't even enjoy spending it anymore. It's all a fake life. I haven't stepped onto my yacht for months..."

"Well, Woody," I offered. "If you will go on this journey with me, and stay with me all sixteen days, maybe you will discover how to find true happiness, and keep it."

"Why can't you tell me your secrets right now?" Woody asked.

"I must show you. We must go to these places, so that your mind will relax, and you can see for yourself what I am saying, with a strong sense of clarity."

"Oh, damn...I've got nothing to lose at this point," he admitted. "I suppose we could take my private jet. Tomorrow morning arrange it with my personal assistant, but don't bother asking her now, since it's Thanksgiving."

"I will do that." I replied.

"How soon will you be ready to leave?" he asked.

I blurted out, "I'll need a week to arrange things with my wife."

Woody nodded. "I probably need that much time myself, to rearrange my calendar. Done." He leaned forward and again I smelled the cigarettes and Scotch on him, as he shook my hand. "Enjoy your Thanksgiving, Carl," he grumbled. Then he turned and walked his lonely path back to his huge mansion...

What Does 'Thanksgiving' Mean to You? Write it down:

_____

_____

_____

_____

That evening, I told my wife of our planned countrywide trip. Since Woody never came back inside, she was worried that he was angry at me, but I assured her that Woody showed up because he needed my help. I expressed how I hated being away from her and our kids for sixteen days, but that I needed to fulfill my promise to the Divine Voice.

The next morning, Rachel, Woody's personal assistant, spent a few hours with me planning trip's details. Since we had a good working relationship due to previously arranging many of Woody's meetings and projects, we easily prepared the itinerary. Our completed proposed schedule and the theme for each stop for all sixteen days included:

Days 1-2:
New York City, New York................................BODY

Days 3-4:
Washington, D.C..MIND

Days 5-6:
Vail, Colorado...WORK

Days 7-8:
Las Vegas, Nevada ....MONEY

Days 9-10:
Mt. Denali/McKinley, Alaska ....GOD

Days 11-12:
San Francisco, California....................COUNTRY

Days 13-14:
Honolulu, Hawaii.......................................FAMILY

Days 15-16:
Los Angeles, California........................FRIENDS

"This is a great idea. Our boss really needs to get away from this place," Rachel acknowledged with a sigh. "He never slows down or enjoys himself."

"So, you believe this trip will help him?" I asked.

"Anything would help," she said. "For almost ten years, I've worked for him and have yet to see him happy. Sometimes I really worry about his mental health."

"I guess he's had poor relationships for a long time."

Straightening her glasses against her oval-shaped face, she sadly disclosed, "The boss hardly knows what a relationship is. I think he was raised under a rock. He does pay well. That's why I've stayed on."

"Woody doesn't mind the cost of the trip, does he?"

Knowing Woody's tastes, at each stop, we had to plan for him to stay at the most luxurious and costly hotels.

"I've witnessed him throw money away on far more questionable ventures," Rachel shrugged, with a stoic voice. "If this puts him in better spirits even for a week, it'll be worth it." She paused and noted, "Since he seemingly owns property just about everywhere these days, so I'm sure our accountants will find a way to deduct most of these costs."

I then wondered, "How much will Rachel's attitude towards Woody change, once he learns the eight values, and puts them into practice?"

Days 1-2: New York City ... Body

It took us nearly a week longer than we had hoped, but finally we embarked upon our momentous journey. Before sunrise, Woody's chauffeur drove us to a private airstrip where his luxurious personal Boeing Business Jet was ready to fly us to our first destination: New York City.

As we boarded his private plane, I told Woody, "Isn't this a wonderful morning? Don't you feel great today?"

Appearing exhausted and slightly hung over, Woody gave me no answer. I could tell he almost said something angry to me, but then resisted the impulse. That was a good sign.

He was willing to let me say things today that he generally considered worthless chatter to him, in his ordinary life. He still wanted to learn how to be happy, so he was giving me some respect.

Shortly after our plane lifted off, a beautiful stewardess served a freshly prepared breakfast. Woody instantly ordered, "Get me a mimosa."

"Isn't this a wonderful experience?" I asked, appreciating the moment. "Imagine how lucky we are just to be here."

Sipping his drink, Woody gave me a slight grin, then leaned back and closed his eyes. Although I felt anxious to talk, I knew I had to proceed with caution. Woody wasn't well-prepared to receive my message. I contained my enthusiasm and forced myself to wait until we landed, before saying anything more.

39

Hours later, after arriving in Manhattan's *Four Seasons* penthouse suite, I suggested, "Woody, let's visit the Observation Deck at One World Trade Center."

"Not before I make some phone calls," Woody snapped, sounding stressed out. "And, answer some emails."

After a couple of hours and several martinis, Woody finally tore himself away from his hotel desk and reluctantly led me to his rented limousine.

Twenty minutes later, when we finally reached the One World Trade Center's top floor, I asked, as we gazed over the broad scene below, "Isn't this a spectacular view of Manhattan?"

"Why are we here?" Woody asked, almost ignoring my statement. "I need a smoke."

"We're here because of this magnificent view," I explained. "Being up here-- seeing so much of the world -- gives you a broader perspective. This is the view of the Divine perspective. God sees how everything works at once. Too often, we exist in our own, little world and think it's the universe."

I continued, "So many of our daily problems that we think are so big and overwhelming are insignificant from the view of the Divine. We worry about little things while forgetting about what truly matters most."

"So, what truly matters?" Woody wondered out loud, while illegally lighting up a cigarette. "What matters most?"

"Your feelings," I replied. "How you feel, as you go through life, largely depends on how much you enjoy your life. Sometimes that's not possible, but when it is, ask yourself why you feel happy. It won't always be the big things you do that will bring you the happiness you seek. It can be small things. But they all have to do with your dealings with people, not with the small tasks that you immerse yourself in. You need to see how what you do, with people, fits into the big picture God has planned for us."

"I don't see any so-called 'plans'," Woody muttered.

"Not if we don't tune in," I told him. "Often, in our work, we push aside our feelings. We ignore our unhappiness. We disconnect from the people we love and from those that we *could* love. We become isolated in our labor. And so, we become even more alone. More depressed. And more disconnected from others.

All because we focus on the little tasks and ignore how we feel about ourselves and those around us. We lose sight of the big picture ... like what we are experiencing right now, looking below at Manhattan."

"The big picture?" Woody mused. Trying to relax, he continued smoking. Sweat started forming on his brow. He mumbled, "So, I should focus less on my small tasks and more on the people around me. Hmmm..."

"You must make a choice to be happy."

"What's that supposed to mean? What kind of choice?"

"I was offered billions of dollars," I told him. "But I realized I'd have to turn it down, in exchange for happiness."

"Billions of dollars?! Who would offer you that?"

I was reluctant to talk about the Divine Voice. Instead, I answered, "I was told that I would find happiness in the other seven values of life. So, I chose them instead."

"So, what are these seven values that you think are so important?"

"That's the purpose of this trip, Woody. To explore all eight values. To fully understand how to incorporate them into your life."

After contemplating my words for several moments, Woody then reluctantly observed, "Yeah, I suppose money means very little, if the rest of your life sucks. So tell me more about the other life values."

"We will discover them, one at a time, throughout the tour. Didn't Rachel tell you about this?"

"Rachel? Who is –" For a moment, Woody had forgotten the name of his long-time personal assistant. He then appeared slightly embarrassed, extinguished his cigarette, and said, "Yeah, well, I trust her in handling such details."

It startled me to see how Woody seemed so detached, even from his personal assistant. I began, "There it is: you trust Rachel. She handles your scheduled needs well. But how do you handle your physical needs? Our first individual value is your **body.** Woody, what is the overall condition of your physical health?"

"Well," Woody began, giving me a very unhappy look, "it's pretty obvious. I'm in bad shape. I've got blood pressure problems. Cholesterol problems. I'm short of breath most of the time. I get stomach ulcers. I need to lose a lot of weight. My doctors warned me that I'm at risk of having a heart attack, if I don't slow down."

Still gazing at the vast and beautiful scene below him, Woody sighed. "I can't relax," he said. "Not without a drink. I drink every day to try to relax. You've seen me eat terrible food. I'm addicted to pastries. Sweets. I know what I'm doing, but it's hard to stop. Hard to change."

"Woody, you must ask yourself, do you really want to be healthy?"

"Of course, I do!" Woody responded, showing some discomfort. "But I'm surrounded by so much stress. So many responsibilities. I chain-smoke. I never exercise – it takes too much effort. All effort is stress."

"You must find your own way to be motivated. Imagine, Woody, how you can become motivated! How can you change your lifestyle! Start imagining what you would like to be!"

"How can I feel motivated, when all I feel is stress?"

"Woody, have faith in yourself! Let's start with basics. Envision yourself as being healthy. The beginning is always difficult because your subconscious mind can betray you. It will tell you 'no.' Not to change. It wants everything to stay the same. But with repetition, you can conquer your problems. Healthy habits are developed by repeating reaffirming optimistic statements."

"That's easy for you to say," Woody remarked.

"Woody, you have to identify the positive events that turn up in your life. Discover your successes. Savor them! And say to yourself, until you believe it: *'Every day, and in every way, I am getting healthier.'*"

"How do I know if I'm making progress?" he asked.

"Grade yourself. Say, from one to five. One is 'poor,' two being 'not good,' three being 'good,' four 'very good,' and five is 'excellent.' How would you grade yourself, regarding your body, right now?"

"Why do you have to do that?" Woody asked, angrily. "You're insulting me! I think it's pretty obvious."

"You must be truthful with yourself. You need to see where you stand," I told him, as he turned away from the huge windows in disgust. "If you're honest with yourself, you will feel the need to change. But you first must *want* to change."

"I **do** want to change," Woody insisted, looking down at his feet. "I can't even see my feet. My belly is in the way..."

Seeing him struggle, his face slightly flushed, I kept silent.

"I know," he admitted, continuing with some despair, "that I am probably at a 'one.' I'm a slug."

"Now, ask yourself how can you move up to a 'two' or maybe even a 'three'? What does it take to accomplish that?"

When Woody stayed silent, I added, "Only you can come up with the right answer. Only you know yourself. Be honest and frank with yourself."

After giving Woody a few minutes of solitude to think about his physical condition, Woody then approached me and suggested, "I could start walking. I can also reduce my smoking and drinking."

"That's a good start! These are the kinds of goals that you need to improve your body. Now, to succeed, I want you to do exactly as I instruct you. Four times each day – in the morning, twice during the day, and before you go to sleep -- tell yourself that your health is getting better and better. Create a slogan. Like, *'Today, I'll make my body better!'* Each day, tell yourself that you will start briskly walking for twenty minutes. Tell yourself that you will smoke less. Write these slogans down on a piece of paper and read them four times a day, until you have them memorized."

"Will that help?"

"Yes. You'll see! Repeat these thoughts with the intense feeling that **you have already accomplished them.**

Believe in yourself! Tell yourself that you are already briskly walking more and smoking less."

"Why do I have to repeat all this?"

"Since our extremely powerful subconscious mind controls most of our actions, you must trick your subconscious mind, which does not know the difference between reality and fantasy, into agreeing that this is not 'change' –it is what you have always been doing."

"So, I can start exercising, stop smoking – whatever – and it's without having to feel the stress? Is that the point?"

"Your subconscious mind will support the new routine, if it will recognize that routine as "not new." It will soon give you good ideas towards fulfilling your goals. By focusing on achievement, you will eventually meet these goals."

"Is it really that simple?" Woody wondered.

Yes, it is. Your own, powerful subconscious mind can help you make it happen. You don't need to know how it works. It just works."

Write Your 'Body'' Slogans. What are your plans?

_____

_____

_____

_____

_____

"Does it come down to, how do I believe?" Woody asked, for the first time showing some enthusiasm.

"Through constant repetition of your slogans, you'll fool your subconscious mind into agreeing with your stated goals. Then, envision yourself achieving your goals."

Woody fell quiet again, as he overlooked the impressive world-class city of New York from its tallest building. Gazing down at the tiny cars on the streets below, he observed, "This hectic city seems quiet, even tranquil, from this height."

Suddenly, his face flushed slightly. "What's the matter, Woody?"

Woody didn't answer; he simply stared at the incredible sight for several minutes while he meditated on what I told him.

Breaking the silence, he confessed, "Carl, I'll try it. I mean, I will **really** try it. I'm not happy about my physical condition. I know I need to take care of my body."

"Woody," I said gently, seeing that he seemed overwhelmed, "you should relax for the rest of the day. Walk around this exciting city and reflect upon what I have just told you. Think about creating your new slogans. Remember, you must write them down. Write them on a note pad. Focus your mind on your goals, as if they were already fulfilled."

I continued, "Before you leave for the day, remember this place. On September 11, 2001, many heroes died here, attempting to rescue thousands of victims. But, we didn't let that day defeat us. We built a more magnificent tower to show the world that the American people will never surrender to terror. Here, standing at the top of this tower, America is a beacon of determination and courage. We've demonstrated that we can overcome obstacles and become even stronger."

Suddenly, I recalled that Woody had some employees who had died there in the flames of September 11.

"Woody," I solemnly said, "don't you realize that you are lucky that you did not perish here on September 11?"

"I actually owned some offices there, had some employees who died there. I'd just canceled a trip to that building, when it happened...'"

"Think about how fortunate you are just to be alive today! Things can change drastically, so enjoy every precious moment. Live life to its fullest each day."

Still trying to absorb my message, Woody awkwardly admitted, "Well, I don't know what to say. I've never heard anything like this. Never thought about such things."

"Before we leave," I added, "think again about your body. What good is anything if we are the reason our body doesn't work anymore? How can you improve your body? You've mentioned some ways."

"I can think of a million ways to not improve my body," Woody answered. "And I don't think much of the latest health fads."

"People will offer you many different ways to deal with improving your body," I answered, "but remember, only *you* know what is good for you. You know it, deep inside, what you should do. For some people, it means eating less or exercising more. Pick what you think is most important for you."

"This is thought provoking," Woody remarked. Sighing, he asked, "Let me see if I understand this correctly? I can create my own formula for my first individual value ... my body?"

"Yes. Create the slogans that best represent your 'body' goals. Repeat them often, so your subconscious mind will accept them as already in place. Then your subconscious mind will use them to help you meet the challenges you face every day."

"Well, uh, OK. 'I will eat with moderation,'" Woody decided. "I will reduce my drinking. Will try to exercise."

"Good! For some people, exercise means walking thirty minutes every day. Others may want to jog twenty minutes. You decide. Be your own judge. Set your own goals."

"Carl, how do I know if this is going to work? How in the hell will I know how long I have to do this?"

"Practice it and watch. Your subconscious mind is capable of many feats. If you feed your mind with wishful action words and repeat them in a spirit of faith and with emotional belief, these goals *will* produce results. They will come true, and your imposed routine will eventually become a totally natural part of your life."

Write Down Your 'Body' Slogans again, and what you plan to do, below...

_____

_____

_____

_____

_____

_____

Now, match what you wrote here with what you wrote earlier. (Did you memorize your slogan and your plan?)

With so much negativity having saturated Woody's mind, he struggled digesting such optimistic thoughts. "Sure, I could use a drink," he admitted, "but I'll hold off. Maybe until dinner. Or maybe, we'll have one tomorrow morning?"

Days 3-4: Washington, D.C. ... Mind

On our third day, we arrived at America's capital. It was a gorgeous, crisp December morning. Soon, our limousine driver arrived, to take us to the Washington National Monument. Once there, as we gazed upward at the huge obelisk, I said, "Woody, Washington is where our individual and collective values can be shaped into the form of greatness and success. This monument symbolizes the city named after the man who founded this country."

"I don't need a history lesson," Woody grumbled.

"Thanks to George Washington and the other founding fathers who crafted the ideals of our Constitution," I replied, determined to get my point across, "we are a free people, living in a country of amazing opportunities."

Warming up to my subject, I added, "Washington envisioned a land free of tyranny, when all seemed hopeless! He fought hard, even at times when it seemed his dream was impossible. He motivated his troops to achieve victory. And, he established and accepted the position of being our first President. Because of Washington's dreams, we have freedom of speech and freedom of religion. Washington's efforts gave us a world vision of human rights, such as our civil liberties, and our right to pursue happiness."

"What does this have to do with my mind?" Woody asked, as we faced the prominent monument that rested on a frost-covered hill.

"Every morning, we face a choice. We can decide to think and to act with optimism, by accepting the most uplifting and positive thoughts, or we can decide to think and act pessimistically by embracing the negatives that pull our emotions down. What is your choice for today?"

"To think positively," Woody confirmed. "But it isn't easy. Is it?"

"It can be. Our thoughts can control us. But we can choose to feed our conscious and subconscious mind with positive and optimistic messages. If we do that enough, we can flush out our negative thoughts."

"Carl," Woody asked, "can you give me some examples?"

"Well, positive thoughts can be based on emotions you have to reach and appreciate, that are within you. Perhaps they have never been reached! But these emotions can be reached by anyone capable of feelings. Your positive emotions exist in those areas of your mind that value love, serving others, creativity, enjoyment, faith, belief, hope, and enthusiasm."

"We're programmed to value those things," Woody commented.

"Be that as it may, these values are centered in your mind, wherever positive thoughts can exist. They can be made stronger and more useful to you. Today, as you know, we are focusing on the second individual value ... our mind."

"Since we have to make a choice," I continued, "let's choose the positive thoughts, just as George Washington did, more than two hundred years ago. Do that by directing your mind to think upon faith, your positive beliefs, your highest hopes ... and don't forget encouragement, enthusiasm, and love."

Write about your most valued positive thoughts.

_____

_____

_____

_____

_____

"Okay, Carl," Woody replied, closing his eyes. "I'm trying..."

"Create slogans again!" I urged him. "Have them reflect these ideas. For your body, you could choose to say, 'Every day in every way, I am getting better and better' or you could say: 'I feel great. I feel terrific. I feel fantastic.' In the same way, you need to create similar slogans, to literally create more positive thoughts for your mind. That is the first step towards improving your mind's entire outlook on life. Your mind will then get healthier."

"I will try," Woody promised. "You know, I haven't had any alcohol since yesterday's lunch. I've already reduced my smoking."

"Good. That's progress for your body. You are visualizing yourself as a healthy person. Now, it's time to make slogans that will help improve your mind. It all runs on the same subconscious principles."

"So, I'm supposed to write down a new set of slogans?"

"Yes. Just as you did for your body, now do it for your mind."

Write down a new set of slogans for your mind.

_____

_____

_____

_____

_____

_____

As Woody got up, intending to start his exercise by walking the length of the Mall, I told him, "It's time we went our separate ways. We can meet again for lunch. In the meantime, enjoy Washington! And as you do, start repeating your old and new slogans. Write the new ones down. Memorize them! Believe in what you are saying. Eventually, you will feel it. Don't give up. Don't let your subconscious mind, which wants nothing to change, try to tell you that you can't improve your mind! With persistence, you *will* succeed. After a while, you will start feeling terrific."

"I'm still not so sure, but I'll try," Woody replied. But just as we commenced to go our separate ways, he asked, "Carl? Are you sending me off by myself because I prefer so much solitude? And why do I need to be alone so much?"

I had to think about that, since I needed very little solitude myself. "Some solitude is important," I told him. "It allows you to know yourself better. It allows you to let go of your conscious worries. To relax. It lets your subconscious mind generate new, fresh thoughts, based on what you have told it. It takes time to do that."

I hoped Woody would someday want to be around people more, but that could take time.

Do you experience too much solitude, or too little? What can you do to achieve balance? Write your ideas here:

_____

_____

_____

_____

_____

_____

Days 5-6: Colorado ... Work

On our fifth day, we flew to the Eagle County Regional Airport near Vail, Colorado, arriving just before lunch. During the jet's descent, we got a view of the magnificent Rocky Mountains and the gondola ski lift that makes Vail so famous. By then, Woody seemed more relaxed than I had ever seen him. He also showed some social progress by occasionally making small talk to me and by acting more polite to his stewardess, Angela.

That afternoon, after arriving at the lavish *Four Seasons Resort* in Vail, (Woody's favorite hotel in Colorado), he announced,

"Carl, I do feel a little better today. I took your advice and repeated to myself those slogans. It seems to be working."

"What happened?"

"I told myself I had done everything I could to prepare for tomorrow, so I could sleep without worrying about it. Know what? I got a good night's sleep! That hasn't happened in a long time."

Not much later, we ascended the mountainside riding the high-speed Gondola One, where we gazed down at the mountain's slopes, garbed with newly fallen snow ... such an amazingly beautiful, peaceful sight!

What surprised me the most was the sparkling resort city of Vail, far below.... Who could guess that the town didn't even exist until 1966 after Pete Seibert and valley rancher Earl Eaton risked everything to create the Vail Ski Resort. The ski resort and its gondola rides didn't just happen. It was because of Seibert and Eaton's hard work and big dreams.

"Now," I began, "today, I will talk about the next topic, which is 'work.' Woody, how much do you like your work?"

"Well, you already know ... I basically hate it," Woody regrettably complained. "I have no enthusiasm. I know the routines to make money, but I don't get along with my employees. They make mistakes I must correct, wasting my time. I'm so sick of my work, but I obviously cannot stop."

Woody sighed. "I even answered forty, maybe fifty emails on our flight this morning. You saw that. Everything feels difficult right now."

"Would you like to know how to change that?"

"Yes, but I doubt you can do anything about it. How can you change the attitude of my employees? You've seen them. Or the amount of work I have to do?"

"Well, list four positive comments about your work."

"There's nothing that I like about my work!" Woody snapped.

"You must search and find the positives. For example, do you own your own business?"

"Of course, I do."

"Do your employees do good work?"

"Of course, because I correct them often and tell them what I want."

"Can you take time off at work?"

"Of course, but only because I own the business ... I could lose it all if I got lazy, so I don't take time off. I worked today. I work every day. It's only a matter of how many hours I work before I collapse."

"Can you delegate problems in the business?"

"Yes, I let my managers handle many problems."

"Now, see? You've already listed four reasons to be happy about your work. You own your business. You have good employees. Your managers handle many problems. You can take off from work sometimes, such as now."

Woody still looked uncertain, so I kept encouraging him.

"Now, think of those positive four things about your business at least four times a day. Try feeling positive about your work. Write down how you can do that."

Write positive notes here about your work:

_____

_____

_____

_____

_____

_____

After Woody wrote down a few sentences, he suddenly said, "I think you're right. I guess I could start by taking a break now and then. I think I should go to my suite and write down some more positive things about my work."

"Woody don't forget! Repeat your slogans with emotion! Reinforce your positive messages with conviction! Write them down and repeat them until you memorize them."

"Yes, I'll do that. I really want to believe this will work."

"Trust me, it will."

Days 7-8: Las Vegas...Money

What a great way to see Las Vegas, landing during a clear evening sky. Below, we saw rows of glittering hotels and amazing buildings dancing with light and colors.

Soon, we checked into an **MGM Grand SkyLoft** villa in the heart of the famous strip in Las Vegas. Before walking down to the casino game room, Woody drank a couple of beers as he tried to relax.

On our flight, he told me how he gambled for years and often won money. He seemed eager to play Blackjack again and quickly sat down at a table before I could begin my talk.

I waited patiently while I watched Woody win over twenty thousand dollars and then gradually lose almost all of it. Stomping his foot twice, he got up and held up a handful of chips.

Mired in a bad mood, he cashed in his chips and muttered, "Carl, what a shit night! Maybe sixteen, seventeen hundred here. That's it!"

He handed me the cash.

"What should I do with this?" I asked.

"Oh, hold onto the change," he mumbled, not seeming to care.

Minutes later, we sat at a table that overlooked an assortment of elegant crystal fountains. As we enjoyed some cocktails, I prepared to begin talking about the value of money when Woody set down his glass and impulsively rushed over to a gaming table. Before I could stop him, he held a $100,000 chip and nearly played it at a roulette table.

"Woody," I warned him, "you aren't here to gamble! You're here to learn the secret to happiness!"

"Happiness is found right here!" Woody replied. "You said we're here to talk about money. This is money!"

"Woody, I can't help you, if you keep refusing to listen to me," I argued, reminding myself to be patient with him. "If you don't want to change, maybe I should go to my room and try again another day."

Gazing at the roulette tables, Woody struggled for a long moment before looking back at me. Very reluctantly, he returned his $100,000 chip and then sunk behind our table.

Overlooking the splendid fountains, as we listened to the soothing sound of running water around us, I explained, "Woody, you are the most familiar with this fourth individual value... money. You certainly have handled much more money than I have. But how much money does it take to make you happy? We all must set individual money goals. Some people are happy with a net worth of $1000. Others may want billions!"

"Like me!" Woody agreed, still struggling to stay in his seat as his eye kept wandering back to the gaming tables.

"Yes.... Well, you must select your own goal. One which matches your desired lifestyle. Each individual has different needs. However, once we create our personal financial goals and achieve them, money then loses much of its importance."

"Not for me!" Woody insisted, "There's no way in hell that money could lose its importance for me," he said, giving me an incredulous look. "How's that possible?"

"Managing your money is a matter of personal responsibility," I told him, "and how you manage it can make you happy, or miserable. Money is supposed to free you from worries, right? It should not become the heart of your troubles. Having enough money can make you feel independent. Being independently wealthy is one way to describe this condition that so many work so hard to achieve."

"Look at what had to happen to create Vail," Woody reminded me.

"It's true that wealth can create a feeling of accomplishment and may increase your self-confidence," I agreed. "And it's true that creating wealth adds to a society's well-being and contributes to developing people's talents and resources for everyone's benefit."

"So, do you value money, or not?" Woody wondered.

"I consider money as a tool," I explained. "It can get things done, but wealth lies in the eye of the beholder. It is relative. And it's not always able to be measured in dollars and cents. Money can be great, but only if, in the final analysis, it contributes to your peace of mind and to the betterment of society. Don't forget that!"

"Of course, spending money fuels the economy," Woody muttered.

"Yes, but if you decide to channel some of your money towards helping others, especially in ways that benefit society in the long run, just make sure you allocate that money to people who are responsible and honest. Think about it."

Write your notes here about your money situation:

_____

_____

_____

_____

_____

_____

"This is very interesting. Kind of inspiring," Woody reflected. "I tend to want to help people, but I don't want them to take advantage of me. I need to learn more about the person's true values before giving them money. You know, I've always noticed that people suddenly 'respect' and 'admire' me whenever they learn of my wealth. But they often don't have any idea of the real me, and my unhappiness."

"Yes, especially if you are weak in the other seven values. But, if you can be successful in all eight values, that will bring you true happiness," I assured him. "So, set your goals. Envision already possessing the money you desire.

Visualize having all the money you want. Then imagine the steps you must take to get that money. Remember, there is no such thing as something for nothing."

"I think I've already used this principle, without realizing it," Woody observed.

"Yes, but if you want your subconscious to help guide you to make more money, then you must repeat your goal. At least four times a day! With fervor! Make your goal become a part of you."

Full of enthusiasm and truly inspired from within, I added, "In sports, many individuals and teams do exactly that, with astonishing results. They receive help from their subconscious minds. Remember, repeating your goal to yourself will sink into your subconscious mind, where it takes hold. You must blend it with positive emotions. In the end, your choices will be wiser because you will trust your gut instincts."

By then, I could tell Woody was thinking deeply about the message. "Carl," he said slowly, "I basically used this formula when I earned my first billion dollars. I instinctively knew what to do."

"I'm sure you did. I think it's what I should be doing, myself, to gain more money, myself," I admitted. "But let's summarize all of this. So far, we've covered the four 'individual' values. Next, we will cover our 'relationship' values. For now, during the rest of our stay in Las Vegas, think of what we have discussed. Write down your slogans. Repeat them over and over. And again, allow them to sink into your subconscious mind."

"How do I know when these slogans or mantras have actually sunk into my subconscious mind?" Woody wondered, scratching his somewhat round chin. "And also, I don't want to get obsessed with something running around and around inside my head."

"You'll know. You'll get a special intuitive feeling from it. You'll start becoming an optimist, because your slogans will be positive, not negative. Once you let your slogans sink in, you'll start feeling changes, because – as I've told you – your subconscious mind will start feeding you with the positive thoughts you've implanted there. It will start directing you on how to obtain your goals. Deep inside, we are all experts at reaching goals. You are, too. You learned to walk. To talk. To take care of yourself."

By the following morning, Woody began working at gaining a good grasp on the four individual principles. He started a habit of summarizing his four values. Next, he picked a slogan for each. He then finalized his choices. For the **body** value he wrote:

"Every day, in every way I eat a better diet."

"I drink less."

"I briskly walk twenty minutes."

"I smoke less."

For the second individual value, **mind,** he picked, *"I think only positive thoughts."*

For the third individual value, **work,** he chose, *"I like my work."*

For the fourth individual value, **money**, his slogan was, *"I will have three billion dollars by next year."*

Think about your own four individual values. Have you memorized them yet? If so, write them down, here:

_____

_____

_____

_____

_____

_____

Days 9-10: Alaska...*God*

Our flight from Las Vegas to Alaska consumed most of our ninth day. During this longer flight, I noticed Woody wasn't spending as much time answering emails. Instead, he was spent much of his of time talking to his stewardess, Angela.

Apparently, she had worked for him for nearly five years, but they rarely talked. Woody also began using a friendlier voice during his phone calls and started paying more attention to other people's needs. Before, he avoided interacting with others, he said, because all too often, they ended up asking him for money.

After we talked about that problem, Woody realized that he could make good things happen to deserving people by helping them anonymously, even making it seem like mere "good luck" had finally arrived in their lives. As time went by, I hoped that Woody's new attitude toward money would eventually make life better for many people. He could do good things for others, in secret. My hope was that seeing the results might make Woody feel a sense of joy he had never experienced before.

What good could you do in secret? Write your notes here:

After arriving in Anchorage, we rested a few hours at a five-star hotel before taking a flight to overlook North America's highest peak, Mt. Denali, which previously was called Mt. McKinley, in honor of the former (assassinated) US President.

I explained that, just as there are many religions, the endless fight to keep changing Mt. Denali's name to Mt. McKinley, or from Mt. McKinley back to Mount Denali, had nothing to do with its truly awesome splendor, or what spirituality was all about.

As we circled the massive mountain in Woody's jet and looked down at its summit, I told Woody, "Today's topic is the spiritual relationship value. Look at this great mountain. Aren't we lucky to see it? Only one out of three days can it be seen, as it's usually hidden by clouds."

"It is breath-taking," Woody agreed.

"Have you ever wondered who created such beauty?" I asked, feeling in awe as I looked down into the huge crags and canyons. "Only God could create such a wonder."

"It must be some kind of a God out there to do such a thing," Woody muttered, genuinely interested. "But when I think of the billions of galaxies out there, it's hard to think that there is a God big enough to care for us, who are so small."

Woody had a point. I'd thought about it myself, many times.

"As I recall," I replied, "We care a great deal about tiny little things that aren't even alive, such as diamonds, which only have monetary value. But can we even guess how much God cares about the spirits He has created? He created them out of the abundance of love He has to give and wants to share."

To this very religious statement, Woody frowned. "I haven't had much love in my life, including from God," he replied.

"Woody? Where are you, on the scale, in terms of your spiritual life?"

"Spiritual life?" Woody laughed. "Well, uh, I don't really have a spiritual life. I hardly know what that means."

"Woody," I reminded him, "you've already begun making good progress with your other three 'individual' values. Your body, your mind, and your work."

"Yes, I feel better. I feel like I am improving."

"That is your subconscious mind working for you. Now, try to discover what you want, spiritually."

After thinking deeply for a long moment, Woody gave me a perplexed look, and finally said, "I think I need some time alone."

Giving him some space, I went to the back of the plane while he continued looking at the magnificent mountain scenery by himself. While I sat in the back, I meditated and prayed that I would find the right words to encourage Woody.

Later, just before we landed back at Anchorage, Woody approached me and announced, "I decided I'd go to the church that I attended when I was a kid. Maybe, I can reconnect with God. Maybe I can even meet some good people there."

"That sounds like a slogan," I replied. "Why don't you write it down?"

Write some notes about your spiritual values here. Can you create a slogan for any of them?

_____

_____

_____

_____

_____

Days 11-12: San Francisco... Country

On our eleventh day, we took a fantastic flight from Alaska to San Francisco. Below, we saw such beautiful countryside that I felt we were inside some masterpiece of a painting. The coastline alone was amazing.

After landing in San Francisco, a chauffeur picked us up and drove us to the famous "lookout point" of Golden Gate Bridge. "This bridge is a landmark, but what does this have to do with the 'country' value?" Woody wondered.

"This bridge represents the diligent efforts of many people working together," I told him. "Working in harmony. There was also a designing team behind the creation of the bridge. They dreamed about the bridge, imagined it, and visualized it in their minds before building it. Relationships are built the same way as bridges. People, working together, in harmony, can create miracles. We all need to ask ourselves, "How can I help and serve my country and our community better?"

"A long time ago, I considered serving the country in the Army," Woody commented. "I thought about it for an hour or so when I was finishing high school. But nobody inspired me. Nobody motivated me. I chose instead to neglect helping the community. All my efforts were for me."

Woody paused and confessed, "You know, I have always resented paying taxes. Furthermore, I never gave to charities, even though it was against my own tax advisors' recommendations. I have never been interested. Maybe that's a mistake. Maybe I should consider ways to help my community."

"When communities benefit, regions benefit. When regions benefit, the country benefits."

When Woody nodded, I was pleased. "I'm glad to see you making more progress!" I told him. "So, Woody, how will you plan to serve your country better?"

"It will take some time. I don't really know that much about Tampa. I'll meditate on it and get back to you, after we return."

"Woody, when we help our country and community, we end up helping ourselves. We can make financial contributions, give of our talents, give of our time.

Ask, 'How can I help make my country and my community stronger?' When your country prospers, you will prosper, too, and you can become more capable of helping others on a personal basis. That starts the cycle all over again. This is what you are doing when you improve your four 'individual' values. You can begin to help make this world a better place, through one act of kindness after another."

"I've noticed how your own acts of kindness makes my staff happier," Woody acknowledged. "But, where do I start?"

"You have to create your own formula because it's your life. Only you can decide when, where and how much to invest in someone, or in something, that will be beneficial. Start with a slogan, such as: 'I will always try to help someone in my community.'

Write your own slogan and thoughts here:

_____

_____

_____

_____

_____

_____

_____

_____

Woody was right: this was one area where I felt I had some real expertise. Encouraged, I told him, "When we help others, we increase our own real happiness, much of it comes from improving our 'relationship' values. But first, before we reach out to help others, we must learn how to help ourselves.

"We must get inspired by the great American spirit of never giving up. And we must be willing to help others, even when we're in a bad mood."

"I'm trying to see what you mean," Woody replied.

"Now, take the rest of the day to think of ways to help society, and how you can possibly contribute. Walk down to Fisherman's Wharf and enjoy the afternoon. Notice the many kinds of people, rich and poor, that crowd the Wharf."

Write your notes here:

_____

_____

_____

_____

_____

_____

Days 13-14: Honolulu, Hawaii... *Family*

On the afternoon of our thirteenth day, we flew over several fantastic islands made from volcanos before landing in Honolulu. I told Woody, as we disembarked, "Today's topic is about our third 'relationship' value, **family.**"

"I wish I had a family," Woody expressed under his breath. "My parents are dead. And I've lost three very short marriages and many more relationships. I just haven't been able to keep any of them going."

Woody's mood was so somber that I knew I had to wait a while before talking about "family" again. Later, as sunset was approaching, we strolled along Waikiki Beach. It was a lonely, beautiful experience.

"Woody, before you think of how you can improve your relationships with the people you care the most about, can we talk more about your family? You never have said much about your family."

Woody was silent for a long time, so we continued walking. I could tell he was uncomfortable. Still, I sensed he wanted to share his past with me but found it difficult to start. He finally said, "My mother left my father when I was very young. I don't know where she went. Dad paid her off and she vanished. But then, they accidentally met again. Things went so well, they planned to remarry ... then came the plane crash."

"That's terrible!"

"Things like that can make you bitter. I guess I just drifted away from what was left of my family after that. There wasn't much to drift away from. I have a couple of cousins in the northeast. There's an uncle in New York." Woody sighed. "But I did hope, someday, that I could have some kids of my own..."

"So, I can see why you would try to make a family several times."

"Tried, yes. Failed, yes."

"Perhaps your slogan should be, 'Try, try again.'"

"Yes, I'm already thinking about starting a relationship with a new woman. I'm not sure if she'll be interested or not. I am not an easy man to live with."

"You won't know until you try. You're making good progress. Create a slogan about it, repeat your slogan, and it will become a reality, with the help of your subconscious mind."

"If I had a family, maybe I could connect better with the community, and with the country," Woody observed.

"Take some time to think about it. I hear there's a nice Polynesian Culture Center on the north end of the island, where you can experience the cultures of the other South Pacific islands out here."

"Relax, learn, and reflect. Right?" Woody replied.

"That's right."

"But why are we in Hawaii?"

"Because Hawaii represents ethnic harmony and the importance of protecting our family values and traditions. President John F. Kennedy said, 'Hawaii is what the rest of the world is striving to become.' In the 1960s, Hawaii's two Asian American senators – WWII veteran and *nisei* Daniel Inouye and Honolulu-born Hiram Fong – helped secure the passage of America's landmark civil rights legislation."

"I didn't know that," Woody said.

"There's more. In 1978, Hawaiian became the official language, along with English, and Hawaii's culture and family traditions were mandated to be taught in all public schools. Today, the whole world enjoys how Hawaii's old ways, and America's modern ways, thrive together in harmony."

Later that night, after enjoying a festive evening watching beautiful women whirling fire batons, and eating delicious grilled seafood on the beach, Woody thanked me for all that had happened to him on this journey so far.

"I see what you mean by finding happiness. I knew there were other values in life besides just accumulating money, but I never thought about taking any time off to experience any of it."

"Money made this present journey possible," I replied, "but you must score high with the other seven values to obtain a well-balanced life."

"Yes, this journey has opened my eyes. Leaving Tampa and getting off the estate has definitely helped me!"

Later, I saw Woody leave the resort to attend another great Luau at the Polynesian center. But he wasn't alone. Angela, his stewardess, was with him. I was pleased. The two seemed to be getting along very well.

It was encouraging to see Woody try to make another emotional connection. Despite all that he had accomplished in the financial world, his family value was the lowest of any of the eight values.

Write here about your own family values:

_____

_____

_____

_____

_____

_____

_____

_____

Days 15-16: Los Angeles ... Friends

On our fifteenth day, we landed in Los Angeles, the City of Angels. It was our final stop before returning to Tampa, and by now, Woody was well rested and really motivated. Though I knew he would be receptive to hearing about the final value, I waited until we arrived in Beverly Hills before beginning our talk.

"California is where we need to speak about the last of the eight values," I told Woody.

"The fourth 'relationship' value concerns what kinds of friends we have. There are four kinds of friends: 'close', 'good', 'social', and 'false'. The close ones walk in when the rest of the world walks out. The 'good' and the 'social' friends are the most common. As for 'false' friends, once you identify them, keep them out of your life. Here in Beverly Hills, Woody, you can easily find 'false' friends, because of your fortune."

"I've already told you about how everybody 'loves' me, the minute they find out I'm rich," Woody remarked. "Most of them wouldn't speak to me, otherwise."

"So, you need to focus on finding out who are your true friends."

"It's hard to know that, when you have so much money," Woody observed. "People always look at that first."

"Try not to always make it so obvious that you have so much money," I told him.

"Remember how we talked about 'giving' anonymously? And take your time. Allow the test of time to determine who is good for you. Don't be a 'rescuer' either. Find out the truth about why somebody is having a hard time. You can't 'save' everybody due to their own choices. Make sure you strengthen your relationships with your true friends, then be there for them. Be happy if you end up with just one or two close friends. Many people don't! Are you ready to create a slogan for this last value?"

Write your notes here. Include thoughts about your best friends, and create a slogan to help you choose true friends:

_____

_____

_____

_____

_____

I knew Woody was concerned the most about this final value.

After all, at least two of his marriages had failed simply because he couldn't determine if either of his wives were true friends or not. From what he told me, they were false friends who mainly liked him for his wealth and not for the person that he was.

I told him, "Think of what kind of a friend you want to be. How would you treat someone yourself, as a true friend? Think of what you would expect from a true friend. It's an old saying, that you should 'Treat your friends the way you would want to be treated.' Remember, friendships are living things! So, cultivate your friendships, like you would cultivate a garden. Don't let them die off from neglect."

<u>Write about how to better cultivate your friends here:</u>

_____

_____

_____

_____

_____

Woody listened carefully. He didn't say a word, but I could tell he was in deep thought over what to do.

I continued, "Woody, now it's time for you to summarize the eight values. Match each chosen slogan with its value."

I handed him a note card and a pen. "Now, see if you can write it all down on a note card."

As Woody began writing, I told him, "When you're finished, put it in your wallet. Copy it into your cell phone. Always keep those slogans with you, much as you can. Look at them frequently, at least four times a day, until you're sure you've memorized them."

Woody agreed. An hour later, after he made some necessary business calls, he finished writing his first complete list of slogans. He wrote:

<u>Value 1</u>: BODY:".........*I will improve my health each day.*"

<u>Value 2</u>: MIND: .... *"I feel great. I feel terrific."*

<u>Value 3</u>: WORK: ....*"I love my employees."*

Value 4: MONEY: ....*"I will have three billion dollars."*

Value 5: GOD: ....*"I will reconnect with God."*

Value 6: COUNTRY: ....*"I will help my community."*

Value 7: FAMILY: ....*"I will make a loving family."*

Value 8: FRIENDS: ....*"I will make great friends."*

Write your own notes here, then transfer them to a note card that you can always carry with you:

_____

_____

_____

_____

_____

After seeing his progress, it was time to show Woody why I was so confident about these goals. I pulled out the magical gold coin from my pocket and placed the coin in front of him on the desk where he had been working. As Woody picked up the coin, admiring its beauty, I said, "Woody, I'm giving you this coin! Even though this coin is my most prized possession, it's not supposed to be mine forever. It's now meant to be yours!"

As Woody held the golden coin and continued to examine it, I continued: "This precious coin will help remind you of your own precious values and what you can do to improve each value. Keep it constantly with you. Look closer at the coin, Woody. What do you see?"

As Woody held the coin closer, he saw the four inscribed action words that had so motivated my own life:

Love – Serve – Create – Enjoy

I continued, "Apply those four words to each and every value. Follow the instructions you have been given, and you, too, will be happy, just as I am happy!"

"I do feel much better!"

"Just remember one thing: *keep on believing!* Then the miracles will come!"

Our two-and-a-half week journey was about to end: time had slowed to a crawl (it had felt like a couple of months). When we finally returned to Tampa, Woody remained true to his word: he began acting like a completely different person in his daily life. Having diligently followed my advice, he began experiencing real happiness and peace of mind. As for Woody's staff, and my wife, they were shocked to see how much he had transformed.

Compared to the man who had left for New York City with a frown on his face, he now seemed to be happy, almost jubilant. And he was coming across as a new man.

I was there when Woody contacted his uncle and cousins on his cell phone. He was reaching out. But Woody didn't stop there: He began calling his staff members by their actual names, rather than referring to them based on their positions. His *"Get your ass over here – I need you!"* bluster was gone. He began attending a church downtown.

And he started regularly dating Angela, the stewardess that he befriended on his private jet.

He even started telling my friends at the café that he had found a new meaning in life, and that his life was incredible. **He had become an optimist.**

What is an Optimist? Write your notes here:

_____

_____

_____

_____

_____

_____

Three Years Later...

Woody's life continued to remarkably change. His efforts to improve the other seven values resulted in a surprise: he realized that he was working fewer hours, but with more efficiency. His manners, and even his English improved, as he studied and learned more about history, culture and people. As Woody became more effective and successful in his business ventures, his wealth increased at a faster rate.

His staff members, due to their boost in morale, were also finishing their tasks more effectively and thoroughly than before.

Through this important time of personal growth in Woody's life, though I mainly worked with Rachel, his personal assistant, I was still eager to encourage and coach Woody whenever it seemed he needed my help. Woody's transformation continued as he turned into a new person. He had quit smoking, except for occasional cigars. He reduced his drinking to a moderate level. He lost almost forty pounds by just doing simple exercises and making a few changes to his diet. There were rumors that Woody and Angela planned to marry. Despite Woody's tremendous progress, I slowly started wondering about my own.

My Turn

The question arose every time we found ourselves needing to fix the old car, or trying to put together enough money for a family vacation. "When will I ever fulfill my money value?" I would ask myself. "When will it be my turn to get help?"

After Woody and I returned from our journey, Sally delightfully informed me that she was pregnant with our third child. Her pregnancy went well -- we were blessed with another beautiful child.

But with three children, my wife could only work part-time. With childcare expenses, it made little sense for her to work. This situation put more pressure on me to find ways to improve my "money value."

The extra savings that we temporarily set aside vanished like smoke with our third baby. Though the other aspects of my life were generally great, once again, I found myself with too little money. I kept remembering the promise of no longer needing to worry about money once I fulfilled my mission to teach Woody the Eight Values on our American journey.

But when would that promise be fulfilled? I waited, but time went by, and nothing happened.

How can you improve your 'money value'? Write your notes here:

_____

_____

_____

_____

_____

_____

A few days before the 3rd anniversary of my trip with Woody, I awoke in the middle of the night, unable to fall back asleep. In the darkness, my thoughts began racing. Sweat formed over my anxious body. For the first time in a while, I felt real despair. While my exhausted wife slept, I felt a tremendous amount of intangible pressure. I didn't know what to do. I got up, wandered into the kitchen, and and paced the floor, feeling overwhelmed.

"Why? Why am I still broke?" I whispered. "Why do I feel alone and unsatisfied? Has the Divine Voice abandoned me?"

As I ruminated in our dim kitchen, I gazed at the stack of bills on our beat-up Formica counter. Not providing for my family deeply disturbed me. The day before, my wife and I had argued over money and our growing bills. Woody's guest cottage, that was once roomy enough, was now filled with five persons –three of them little children. For the first time, I began imagining not working for Woody.

I wanted my own home, and a better-paying job. As I walked the floor, I even more grew puzzled and confused over my uncertain sense of direction in life.

"Didn't I complete my task?" I asked, in a whisper. How could the Divine Voice let me fall into this situation? Then I pleaded to myself. "Why am I not making more money?"

What is preventing you from making more money? Can it be fixed? Write your notes here:

_____

_____

_____

_____

I felt that I could ask Woody for a raise, but really, he didn't need me anymore. Besides, he was already paying me more than the "prevailing market" for most of his staff members, because I had to support a family.

And Sally was ready for a change, too. For the first time, my wife suggested that she did not look forward to living in the guest cottage with four children to keep track of, on someone else's property. I knew she longed for a place of her own.

Then Thanksgiving Day arrived.

Once again, we hosted a big dinner for many of our friends and some of Woody's staff members. This year, they brought some food dishes of their own. Later that afternoon, Woody and Angela showed up for dessert. Bursting with happiness, she had finally introduced him to her parents earlier that day.

Woody arrived at our guest cottage beaming with joy. With his arm around his happy girlfriend, he announced to everyone, "Angela and I have decided to get married!"

Everyone clapped. We had a congratulatory toast. The cottage was filled with happy people ... except for me.

After a half hour or so of socializing, Woody began noticing my troubled condition – another sign of the tremendous progress that he had made with his relationship values. He could tell that my usual positive, outgoing behavior was subdued and somewhat somber. Even my wife reflected a cool attitude, as she was also negatively affected by me.

"You prepared another superb Thanksgiving feast," Woody told my wife with a broad smile on his delighted face. "Even with the new baby! I'm impressed!"

My wife was happy, but feeling my insecurities, she struggled to show as much enthusiasm as she would have liked. She managed to reply, "Carl and I always wanted a big family. We love children."

Woody gave a nod, then motioned me to follow him outside. As we began briskly walking around his vast estate, I was impressed with Woody's progress for the body value. Three years ago, he would have wanted to quickly sit down on the nearest bench to rest.

"My thoughts are often clearer when I go for these walks," Woody commented. "You know, I never walked around much on my property until I started doing these hikes. I didn't even realize we had deer, raccoons, and even alligators here."

"You've made tremendous progress," I assured him, trying to conceal my own concerns by acting positive.

"Carl, what's the matter? You seem troubled."

"Woody, time is passing me by, to be frank with you."

"What do you mean?"

"I feel confused about my life. I'm not doing so well with the money value. My bills are piling up. I was able to help you, but I can't seem to help myself. And I don't want more money from you, for my kind of job here. I need to get back to the kind of work I love... running a café, for example..."I continued, "My wife and I are beginning to argue over money."

"We all argue over money," Woody bluntly replied. "I've had money fights with my three previous wives. If I marry Angela, as I plan to, I'll probably at some point argue with her about money."

"Yeah, but Sally and I've never really done that before," I told him.

I heard resentment in my tones. I was losing my optimism! "Remember, how I told you about the Divine Voice?" I queried.

"Of course," Woody replied. "It was the beginning."

"Well, the Voice promised me that I'd have true financial success if I fulfilled my part. I thought I did what I was supposed to do, but now I've even lost all my savings! And look how much time has passed! Three years! I must have been doing something wrong, Woody, but what? Haven't I fulfilled my promise?"

As I continued, my voice became more elevated, "And now, we have a fourth child. My wife had to quit working altogether because childcare costs too much. She'll be completely dependent upon me."

"I see what you mean."

Woody pondered my comments for a long moment. As we neared one of the picnic tables on his property, I was the one who wanted to sit down. Then Woody began to speak on the value that had brought him such success. His voice rang out with the same tone of authority that I had used with him three years earlier. It was now his turn to teach me, for making money was his forte!

"Financial responsibility begins with you," Woody told me. "Your expectations after our American trip were very high. But our behavior is often governed by natural dynamics. Such as, 'as you sow, so shall you reap' or 'for every action, there is an equal and opposite reaction'."

"But how does that relate to me making more money?" I asked.

"It seems you thought you had to wait for the Divine Voice to offer you the right opportunity," Woody replied.

"True."

"But what if you are supposed to make your own opportunities?"

"Well, Woody, what actions should I take, then?"

Woody mused over my question, then replied, "Carl, I've often thought about how I could help you. I know you can't stay in your current job forever. You've outgrown this position. And you are gifted in running something service-oriented, like a nice cafe. But I think you need to get a better understanding of what caused this money issue, before taking the next big step in your life."

"What do you mean?"

"It's your turn, my friend, to go on a great journey. But this time, I will be your mentor, and you will be my pupil."

"How did you happen to think of that?" I asked, genuinely surprised.

"I've thought about having this talk with you for a long time," Woody confessed. "At first, I wanted to give you some big reward, for all you have done for me, but something in my thoughts seemed to keep saying, 'Wait! He's not ready!' Maybe you could call it your Divine Voice."

"Well, I'm ready now!"

"Okay," Woody said. "Then here's how it will go. We will make eight stops."

"Eight, like on our first trip? Why?"

"But this time, outside the United States. Each place will present you with new messages and images that you've needed to help teach you what went wrong. Why you failed to make enough money."

Woody then opened his wallet, reached into it, and drew out his golden coin. Placing it on the table, he said, "Carl, I've practically been ordered to help you understand the 'money' value, by some force I can't explain."

"I'm well aware of how that feels."

"We have to act on what is revealed to us," Woody explained. "Money problems are ruining your happiness. The magical principles that brought you everything good – except making money – must be properly utilized to reach your last important goal: making money. Learning how to realize that goal will require your full attention, an intense commitment."

"So, we must go alone again? Without our families?"

"Just as it was for me, you will need to concentrate on this issue with fewer distractions. So, I think we should put ourselves in the same situation as before."

"Okay, I'll find a way to tell Sally and the kids," I replied, feeling a twinge of enthusiasm. I had hardly left the Tampa Bay area in the last three years. At the very least, such a journey could temporarily ease my troubled mind, even though my absence would put a burden on my wife.

"Carl," Woody announced, "this may surprise you, but the trip is already prepared."

Smiling at my astonishment, he added, "During the last month, Angela and I have been secretly organizing a detailed journey around the world. For weeks, I've felt pressure here –" Woody tapped his chest – "that it was time. Time to help you with the money value."

"Yes, I do need help," I mumbled. "I've felt lost."

"This voyage will help you recapture what you lost."

"Where will this journey take us?" I asked.

Woody reached inside his jacket and drew out a thick gold envelope. "The details of the eight stops are in here."

"I hope Sally and the kids will understand. I won't be here to help."

"Your wife knows that you need to make a change. She knows your whole family will benefit from this." He paused, then said, "Go ahead. Open the envelope."

My nervous hands tore open the golden paper. Inside was a print-out of a list of hotels, cities, and details of activities.

World Journey Itinerary:

Stop 1:......................**Bali, Indonesia**

Stop 2:......................**Shanghai, China**

Stop 3:......................**New Delhi, India**

Stop 4:......................**Cape Town, South Africa**

Stop 5: ....**Berlin, Germany**

Stop 6: ....Paris, France

Stop 7: ....London, Great Britain

Stop 8: ....Rio de Janeiro, Brazil

My heart raced with excitement. I felt hope again, for the first time in months.

"Each place," Woody assured me, "will help you focus on one 'magic' word. There are eight of them."

Seeing my puzzled face, he added, "Carl, learning how to tap into the magic of these eight words may not happen immediately. But as we progress on this important journey, you will see how the principles they teach can generate monetary rewards."

"Why must we travel so far? Why can't you teach me right away?"

"If you remember," Woody replied, "I asked you the same question before our previous journey. Removing yourself from familiar places helps you form new ideas and new habits. You'll be inspired. Motivated. Each site possesses a special message. You can give Sally the itinerary in that golden envelope," he went on, "but the next item I want to give you will be for your private use." He handed me a rolled-up scroll. It seemed old – ancient. As I unfolded the yellowed parchment, I noticed the words had been written with letters that looked archaic and strange.

"It's a copy, in a more modern language, of a very old document," Woody explained. "I spent a lot of money to obtain the tattered remains of the original."

"Don't think I'm crazy," he added, seeing the puzzled look on my face, "but when I was told about the legend, I grew excited. Something, from somewhere, was inspiring me!"

To my confused look, he said, "Do you remember how that eagle dropped the coin in your hand, and then a 'Divine Voice' began to talk to you?"

"I'll never forget it."

"The story behind how this scroll came to be is very similar to your own experience," Woody said excitedly. "It says a mighty eagle flew in from a starry sky and dropped this scroll at the feet of young King Solomon, who had prayed not for power, or for fortune, but for the wisdom to guide his people. That pleased God, not only made Solomon the wisest man in the world, but also the richest. Who hasn't heard of King Solomon's mines?" Woody smiled. "Of course, it's only a legend..."

As I stared at the scroll, which I held in trembling hands, Woody said, "Go ahead. Read it out loud."

The Eight Magic Words

1. Attitude

2. Goals

3. Repeat

4. Prioritize

5. Think

6. Serve

7. Honesty

8. Gratitude

After I finished reading the "'magic" words, Woody observed me cautiously, trying to evaluate how I was digesting the information. I then said with a firm voice, "Okay. When do we leave?"

"We'll leave as soon as we can."

Unlike the previous trip, Sally wasn't so eager to let me go. After all, we had two little kids, plus a toddler. But she sensed my unhappiness and my need for motivation and inspiration.

In her eyes, I saw how much she would miss me as I said good-bye to her and our children.

Despite my initial excitement, I also felt some anxiety. This was my first overseas trip. Part of me couldn't wait to jump aboard Woody's newest Boeing Business Jet to experience the world and discover its many messages, but part of me was reluctant, even scared. It wasn't easy to simply leave your loved ones to embark on a global journey with no exact return date, but I trusted Woody's ability to teach me his money-making secrets.

Over the past couple of years, I had noticed Woody reading many self-help books. I also would catch him listening to inspirational podcasts and watching streaming videos.

The result was that he had transformed himself into someone whose advice I could trust.

Do you trust yourself? Write your notes here:

_____

_____

_____

_____

_____

Eight Days Later...

We boarded Woody's Boeing Business Jet, destination: Bali, Indonesia. After settling down, I realized Woody had brought Angela along to accompany us. Startled, I asked, "Didn't you say you wanted us to be alone on this trip?"

"I said we should do the same as we did last time. Angela was with us last time, but Sally wasn't," Woody replied, smiling. "And after all, since she's going to be my wife, she should learn about the money value as well."

Woody, who could still sense some discomfort and tenseness in me, then added some magic words of his own.

"After you have learned these secrets," he said, "I'll be glad to help you and your wife go on that vacation you've wanted to take for so long! I'll get you a nanny, so don't worry about that! Then you can get Sally to think about the money value, too. Consider it my Christmas gift to both of you."

All I could do was to thank him for such a great gift.

On our way to Bali, we made three brief fuel stops in Los Angeles, Hawaii, and the Philippines.

During those flights, Woody spent much of the time alone with Angela or was largely quiet around me. He told me to think of what I wanted to do with my life regarding earning money. He said I should focus on that, and to clear my mind from other concerns.

<u>Focus on what you want to do in your life regarding earning money. Write your notes here:</u>

_____

_____

_____

_____

_____

_____

During those flights, I enjoyed the amenities onboard, especially the media center and the Jacuzzi tub. After playing a game of billiards with Woody on the gyro-operated table, I rested on a chaise lounge, snacking on the health food Woody now preferred to eat. After that, I simply gazed out the window at the clouds below.

As our flight neared its end, my sense of excitement started to build. I wondered, "What will Woody teach me?" Then, I fell asleep...

Stop 1: Bali, Indonesia... Attitude

"Carl," Angela announced, politely awakening me, "we will soon land on the gentle, spiritual, enchanted island of Bali."

"I've never left America," I confessed, still feeling sleepy. Within seconds, as my adrenaline started to rush, I added, "I can't wait to see this marvelous place!"

"It *is* a marvelous place," she agreed. "Woody has gone here several times. Many people say Bali is the place where visitors refuse to leave. Sometimes, the tourists even destroy their return ticket."

She smiled, then handed me a small stack of travel books. "Woody wants you to read these. Each book covers one of the eight places we'll visit. I think you'll like them."

Minutes later, I buckled up as we started our descent to Bali, where a magnificent landscape, filled with lush, green rainforests and volcanic mountains, came into view.

It was like another planet. As Woody's pilot announced that we were approaching Denpasar International Airport at Bali, I thought, "What an incredible experience!"

Soon, we stepped from the plane, where we were greeted by a group of gentle, charming Balinese. Woody had arranged to have them meet us. They seemed to have perfected the art of welcoming the world, yet they appeared to have retained their own culture and distinct values.

Two of Woody's Balinese employees soon arrived, who escorted us to a waiting limousine. It whisked us away to the manicured grounds of The Four Season's Resort at Jimbaran

Bay. As we approached Four Seasons, we enjoyed a broad view of the gorgeous Jimbaran Bay, shining an intense blue.

As we stepped from the limo, we were welcomed by two smiling Balinese valets who led us inside the palatial resort.

"I can't believe I'm here. In Bali!"

A week before, I hardly knew the place existed.

The dazzling sight now stretching out before me was almost overwhelming.

The elegant hotel, which overlooked the ocean, featured rich, exotic Balinese architecture in its lobby, glowing against a panorama of blue and green, beyond which lay traditional pagodas. Soft music was playing, and trays of refreshments awaited us.

Next, we were escorted to Woody's private Four Seasons resort villa, which included its own spa and plunge pool.

Despite being affected by jet lag, we were all eager to see the new and stimulating sights. The immense beauty of it kept me completely alert and awake.

I was soaking in all the beautiful details in the hotel gardens and appreciating all the considerate service offered by the friendly staff. I could hear the waves, smell the refreshing mountain air. A calm, peaceful atmosphere surrounded us.

"Woody, this is amazing! Everyone here is so friendly."

"This is the perfect place for our first lesson, **attitude**," Woody replied. "It is the first magic word you need, in order to succeed. Next, we'll visit Ubud, central Bali's spiritual mountain village."

After a few hours of rest, Ari, Woody's driver, took us to Ubud. As he navigated the lushly green roadway, I gazed at the sights from our limousine, observing the Balinese people in their thatched huts and villages. Their lives seemed simple and slow-paced, so different from American city life! We finally stopped near the carved stone gates and wooden walkways of Ubud's sacred Monkey Forest Sanctuary. There, we were entertained by a ring of exotic dancers in bright-colored costumes, moving hypnotically to exotic music.

Woody grinned. "See all these beautiful people? See their friendly, positive way of doing things? See how their culture reflects their peacefulness"?

We were witnessing a Bali Barong Dance with the rhythmic Gamelan Orchestra. After that outstanding performance, we debarked down one of the mystical trails leading into Ubud's Monkey Forest. Since Angela stayed in the limousine, helping with Woody's emails, we soon found ourselves standing alone in the depths of a silent forest. There, inside the park near the temple, Woody started explaining his message, despite my being distracted by the chattering monkeys. One of them even jumped on my shoulder and grabbed a bag of peanuts from my hand!

"Carl, here we are…" Woody said, as I watched the monkey swing up into a tree and begin munching on my peanuts, "… clearly in a different culture, on the other side of the world! Why do you think we have traveled so far?

"I'm not sure."

"Well, it's because the Divine Voice told me to."

"What? Did the Divine Voice also speak to you?!"

"Not in the same way as to you," Woody replied.

"But remember, I had your gold coin. And I could feel the powerful flow of its message, every time I held the coin in my hands. It was finally made clear that I had to speak to you about the impressions I received."

"If it wasn't for that gold coin, I wouldn't have believed a word you're saying!" I told him.

"Well, quite some time after those first impressions, over a year after you gave me the coin," Woody went on, "a Divine Voice finally broke through the barrier of resistance I had about "spirituality." When I finally gave up, and started listening, the Divine Voice began to speak more clearly to me."

"Does your analyst know about the Voice you're hearing in your head?" I asked. "They have remedies for that, you know!"

"You know damned well," Woody said, "that this Voice is totally different from anything I could have imagined. Anyway, by now, I was ready to listen ... and the Divine Voice began to tell me that someone would '**ask, seek, and knock**. That someone would want to know how to become wealthy. Not because of his own desires, but because he wished to help his family and others to have a better life. I knew the Voice was talking about you."

Woody's voice sent a chill down my spine, as he told me, in a deep whisper, "The Voice gave me a choice: to do this service for you, or my personal goals would not be fulfilled. I felt obligated."

Woody then led me farther down the trail through the trees, which opened to a panoramic view of the rice fields below. In the distance, we could see more terraced green rice fields, arching up the hillside. As we walked toward them, I felt a unique, peaceful sensation.

"Making money isn't just about hard work, or every slave would be rich," Woody began. "In fact, making money is an art, and managing money is a science. You must master both."

He led me down past several terraced rice fields, where we observed the determined, hard-working farmers tilling the soil. They seemed to toil harmoniously with their land. In the distance, I heard roosters crow. As we inhaled the incredibly clean, fresh tropical air, we admired the misty valley below.

At that point, as my emotions resonated in an state of equilibrium and tranquility, Woody asked, "Are you ready for the first word?"

I said, "Okay. I feel ready."

Woody's voice went down to a whisper as he said, "The first magic word is '**attitude**.'"

"**Attitude**," I repeated.

"Yes, your attitude. It stands and falls with the results you seek to obtain. A positive attitude creates good results. A negative attitude generates bad results."

"That sounds reasonable. But in the past, I had such a great attitude towards all parts of my life. I even taught you how to use positive thinking."

"Yes, I remember," Woody responded. "But then, what happened to you, three years later?"

"I guess I did not keep up with the message. I slacked. I realize now that I can't do that."

Do you have a habit of slacking? Write your notes here:

_____

_____

_____

"Why did you become slack?"

"I didn't consistently maintain a positive **attitude**. When the Divine Voice first presented the message, I chose to follow His command to always repeat positive thoughts, in every and all situations. It worked. Then I had it all. Except money."

"Lacking money was holding you back, wasn't it?"

"Yes. As my responsibilities to work and family increased, not having enough money began to weigh on me. I felt I was letting down my family. And nobody, outside my family, cared how hard I worked, without getting ahead financially. It was a big negative in the positive life I was trying to lead."

Throughout this conversation, we kept walking, and now the scenery had changed: we had reached the valley's lowest place. Before us was a vast, brown, dried-out rice field. It reflected my sad feelings. As we gazed at this dry rice field, Woody asked, "So, with that state of mind, what happened?"

"I forgot to repeat all my positive reinforcements," I admitted. "That allowed negative thoughts to invade my mind. I began to feel worry and fear. Even panic."

What negative thoughts are bothering you? Write your notes here:

_____

_____

_____

_____

_____

With all the beauty that had once surrounded us, here we stood, standing in the middle of a bumpy dirt road, staring at a dried rice field. There seemed to be no clear path back to the beautiful, green woods that we had left behind.

"Carl," Woody offered, "I brought along a sheet of paper. As you stand here, at the lowest place, write down the eight magic words again. Writing them down will always help you focus."

Almost frantically, my hand scribbled them down: *Attitude, Goals, Repeat, Prioritize, Think, Serve, Honesty, Gratitude.*

As I wrote, using my knee for a table, I saw Woody's thick hand subtly reach down into his coat pocket. Then he held up the gold coin that I had given him on our previous journey. In a hushed voice he said, "Here we are, halfway around the world, twelve time zones from Tampa. Thanks to this coin."

I folded the paper, shoved it into my pocket, and reached out to touch the rim of the shiny coin, but as I tried to clutch it in my hand, somehow the coin slithered from my grasp and landed on the ground.

"Carl, pick it up again! Take hold of it!"

I quickly took up the coin again, this time gripping it hard.

As I did so, suddenly, the Divine atmosphere began to reappear. stronger and more intense with every moment, causing my thoughts to swim. I was being immersed in an immense sea of cosmic relaxation, while my mind glowed with an incredible feeling of enlightenment. A cascade of ideas began to flow, creating a glowing kaleidoscope of thoughts across my mind.

"This first stop ... Bali ... incredible!" I managed to say. "I do feel spiritual. This is truly a magical place."

"Back when you first had me think of the God value," Woody replied, "this was the place I thought of first."

"I see what you mean."

We fell into silence as an aura of peace and contentment grew within me. Finally, Woody took the coin from me and put it back in his pocket, giving me a smile. "Let us return to the Gate now," he said. "And as we walk, focus on **attitude.** It is that simple, Carl. Every morning, every day, and throughout the day, you will find yourself making choices. Either handle them by embracing positive, uplifting thoughts, or let negative, destructive thoughts drag you down. You do have a choice."

"I see what you mean." He continued, "You see, when you step into the world of the positive attitude, you're given power. You're helped, I'm helped, the people in your community are helped, and the whole world benefits."

I thought about Woody's words. I knew that each day, as our powerful technology makes our world smaller, that even my choices might make a difference. Only time would tell.

<u>Write some positive thoughts here:</u>

_____

_____

_____

_____

_____

Spotting Angela seated in a restaurant not far from the Gate, we joined her at a beautiful-lacquered table, where we ordered some amazing food. "Look at us!" Woody exclaimed. "Here we sit, thousands of miles away from Tampa. Yet, we are still so close!"

He snapped a photo of his food. "Yes, we are so close to everybody now, in the sense that I can readily use my satellite phone or my wireless internet connection to contact anyone in the world, in moments. I can even show them what I'm eating, right now."

"That is so true."

"You see, Carl, a positive **attitude** is infectious. It can potentially influence millions. Practicing good attitude will serve you well in all situations in life. You can feel this **attitude** with the good people here in Bali. The Balinese all seem to smile perpetually. Happiness seems to radiate from their souls, through their smiles."

"I have to agree."

"When you encounter such positive energy, you can't help but return a smile," Woody said. "Just like a yawn, a smile is infectious! Now, what I want you to do is to try to concentrate, on channeling your positive emotions into your intellectual mind. Not thoughts. Emotions."

"I'm not sure how to do that."

"Think positively, as often and as much as you can, towards supporting the activities and people that you value most in life."

"Not easy, if you're depressed," I reminded him.

"That's why you must reject the negatives you feel! It's the great secret that every successful salesman uses. A positive approach, using communication, can shape and re-enforce a positive mental foundation. That affects your emotions and will lift them."

"Oh, the subconscious..."

"Yes. When continually utilized, this paves a positive **attitude**. With a positive attitude directed to your subconscious, that will extend far beyond yourself, for the world to see and enjoy."

"But the world doesn't see or enjoy what I do," I countered.

"Consider what you're saying," Woody replied. "When the world receives positive energy and expressions from you, you will find that it will reflect that positive energy back to you, in ways unimaginably rewarding."

Woody nudged my shoulder. Through the restaurant window, he had spotted some young Balinese people walking down a path toward the rice fields.

"They are in no rush to get there," Angela observed.

"There is no reason to rush," Woody told us. "We need to understand that, when dealing with them in business, those young people are all potential friends, suppliers and customers. Those people could be working for us. Or buying from us."

Woody glanced at his voice-activated Rolex. "We must head back to our villa, but I suggest that you extend your visit in the Kuta Village. Walk around. Take your time. Take this walk alone. Try absorbing the tranquility of this place. Watch the beautiful sunset. Hear the music – observe the dancing! Take a taxi back to the hotel," he said, handing me some money. "We must go now."

I was soon outside again, headed for the village with its round buildings and thatched roofs. As I walked. I thought, "It is important to develop and apply a positive **attitude** with everyone I meet. And even if I never see them again, I can still pretend that I actually *will* see them again!

I recalled Woody's statements about my existing 'assets.' I had two: my precious time, and my marvelous mind. Together, they represented the boundaries of my potential in life.

"They may appear limitless at first," Woody had told me, "and they aren't often effectively used. Further, it's rare that they are efficiently used. And they don't last forever." It was a lesson I had to really think about.

I still felt helpless, seeing no clear way to make more money. Greatly concerned, I entered a Kuta coffee house and ordered some Java coffee. As I sipped it, I meditated on the word **attitude** and what it meant to me. The coffee's rich, strong taste and aroma soothed my mind.

Then I strolled around Kuta's open market and small outdoor shops, pondering Woody's words. For hours, until shortly before sunset, I walked around, smiling, greeting the people, enjoying creating simple interactions with the friendly people around me. But then, as the sun began to set, I fell into silence, focusing on trying to enhance my creative thinking.

At Kuta Beach, I stood entranced, transfixed by the crimson-edged clouds, with the deep blue sky turning slowly darker as the roar of the sea-waves pounded in my ears.

The sunset was seductive. I was almost hypnotized by it.

After the sun sank into the ocean at Kuta Beach, I walked slowly back to the street and found a taxi.

The friendly Balinese driver, Katut, showered me with questions about America. He began by asking why I was visiting Bali. By the time Katut dropped me off at Woody's villa, I clearly saw the truth in Woody's emphasis on **attitude.** I knew now that if I smiled and kept a positive attitude towards all people and situations, the world would return the smile to me. And I would feel peace. It was really that simple.

Before I got into to my comfortable bed at Four Seasons, I thanked God, grateful for these mind-opening experiences. I was learning some very simple, powerful truths. They had always been available to me, if only I would take the time to feel them, not just think about them. I couldn't wait to see what tomorrow had to offer.

How much peace of mind do you have? How can a positive attitude help you?

_____

_____

_____

_____

_____

Stop 2: Shanghai, China... Goals

My Bali experience was so different from my usual life that I had trouble falling asleep. It seemed only moments before Woody was there, fresh and ready to go, nudging me awake.

I stumbled out of bed, packed my clothes, got on Woody's plane, and promptly fell asleep again.

Soon enough, I awoke. With a fresh smoothie made by Angela in my hand, I sat down next to Woody. Looking down from the jet's window, I gazed upon a seemingly endless number of skyscrapers, crowded together. The skyline was surreal!

"Carl, that's Shanghai," Woody told me. "The great Chinese metropolis!"

"It's – huge!!" I exclaimed, never having imagined that a city of such a magnitude could exist.

Soon, we safely landed at the ultra-modern Hong Qiao International Airport. Our Chinese chauffeur, Lee, then drove us to the Portman Ritz-Carlton Hotel located on Nanjing Road. At its entrance, we crossed an arched bridge which extended over a fish-filled pond.

At check-in, we were given impeccable service by the smiling, attentive Chinese staff.

As the elevator brought us toward the Presidential Suite, I exclaimed, "Woody, I can't believe we're seeing modern China! I've read so much about this fascinating country. I can't wait to see the sights, like the Chenghuang-Miao Temple."

"Yes," Woody said enthusiastically. "But first, we'll go to the top of Shanghai Tower, which is one hundred and twenty-eight floors high. We'll have lunch inside its rotating restaurant, then take its elevator — one of the world's fastest — to its Observation Deck, which is the highest on earth. There we'll view this marvelous city's many sites, so you can feel the real pulse of Shanghai."

"Why did you choose Shanghai?" I asked.

"Because, right now, this is the most upbeat city in Asia. Also, to talk about our second word, **goal.**"

Woody smiled. "The example of Shanghai will show you how to make more money. To discover truth, you must keep an open mind. You must search for it. Sometimes, it is found in new frontiers. Now, let's eat lunch!"

At lunch, Woody revealed that he had made many lucrative business deals in Shanghai. "I needed a secretary with me to keep the names straight," he confessed, looking at Angela. "From now on, that is going to be you," he told her. "By the way, the ten most popular names here are Zang, Wang, Zhu, Zhou, Wu, Xu, Shen, Chen, Li, and Lu. If you can keep that straight, you will be worth your weight in renminbi."

"What is that?" I asked.

"The Chinese currency is known as renminbi -- 'the people's money.' Better known as the RMB."

Woody's speech reminded me that he was an excellent businessman who always took time to know the terminology, the correct customs, and the right names. After enjoying a delicious meal, made special because Woody knew exactly what to order, Woody continued his lecture.

"We must talk about goal setting," he insisted. "Look at this city from up here! The government of Shanghai set up a **goal** to become the economic and financial center of Asia. And they made it happen. Why do you think it happened?"

"Because they motivated the people."

"Good. Now, Carl, what do you love to do?"

I hesitated, not knowing immediately what to say. I finally muttered, "I have a passion for helping people."

Woody nodded, patiently.

"Maybe," I continued, with an uneasy voice, "Maybe I could own my own company?" So many questions and ideas were spinning around in my head.

"Well, Carl, what do you **most** desire to do?"

After a lengthy silence, I confessed, "Woody, my mind is filled with ideas. Way too many. But if I really consider everything I want, my deepest desire is to own a restaurant like Joe's Café. But how could I pull together the money to buy a place like that?" (Woody knew I was too proud to accept any big money from him!).

"Sometimes people treat their wishes as mere daydreams," Woody replied, "thinking they can't make their dreams come true. So they simply don't follow through. They won't set a goal and make a committed decision because that takes effort, discipline, consistency, and dedication to make it real."

"We're taught that we shouldn't have an obsession," I argued. "And if we fail, maybe we've wasted our life."

"But sometimes people impose big limits to their wishes, fearing big losses, and then decide not to try. Try not, succeed not."

I gulped down the last of my warm Chinese tea and suddenly looked at Woody. "Okay, Woody," I said, steadily, "I want to buy Joe's Café from you."

"That's a good start! Now to do that, you need to do some research. How much income can you earn from the restaurant? How much would you expect to make within the next three years? Have you considered creating multiple sources of income?"

"I'll have to work on that."

"Carl, you do realize it doesn't matter to me if you quit working for me, because as your true friend, I will welcome your committed decision to follow your passion and fulfill your dreams! Now that you've decided on your **goal** – to own the café – consider how you will manage to do it."

"It's not a small matter," Angela said.

"I know that better than anyone," I told them.

"But big or small, every company consists of four major compartments," Woody went on. "You must pay attention to all four. Find ways to improve your effectiveness in each."

Woody handed me another piece of paper: "Read it out loud," he commanded.

- **FINANCIAL:** In three years, how much income and wealth will you have? How many multiple sources of income will you have in the next three years?

- **PRODUCTION:** Imagine what goods and services you will produce in your new business or businesses? How will you operate or manage the production process?

- **SALES:** Imagine how much your sales will be in the next three years? How many customers will you serve? How much product will you sell? How will you make your sales? How many people will be selling for you? Where and what will you sell?

- **RESEARCH:** What will you research? How much time will you spend on research? How much of your total revenue will you allocate towards research?

"I stress that good performance in all four categories is necessary to achieve a profit and to stay profitable," Woody said. "Listen to the voice of experience!"

"I'm lucky to know such a financial expert," I replied.

"It seems I was brought into your life to teach you what you need to know about making money," Woody replied. "Even so, you must be willing to be teachable. And committed to finding solutions to improve your business operations and your competitive position in your market. You need to learn how to identify what wastes money, exert leadership, guide your team and apply practical systems that will work best for your whole team."

"How do I even begin?" I asked.

"You have a head start. You were the general manager. You already know a lot about running Joe's Café. Intensely study your field of interest, your job, your company, and its people. When we visit the other places, I will tell you more. Remember, when you select a purpose, based on a vision, you must create a plan to generate multiple sources of income for yourself."

"How do I make multiple sources of income?"

"Form partnerships. Consider the many ways that money is made in your occupation."

"Aren't you supposed to concentrate on one activity and do that well?" I asked.

"No," Woody said. "You can maintain all your MSI eggs in one basket if you watch them carefully."

"What's that?"

"Management, Strategy and Innovation. Remember that every business owner has the capacity to earn multiple sources of income. Make it part of your **goal.**"

"You're right!" I said. "I see it now."

"Write your stated financial objective. You want a specified net worth. Set a date to fulfill each **goal.** Write down your planned actions on a worksheet."

What is your big dream?

_____

_____

_____

Can your dream earn an income?

_____

_____

_____

_____

Can you create multiple sources of income to finance it? List some possibilities here:

_____

_____

_____

_____

Do you have the ability you need, or must you get more education in the field?

_____

_____

_____

_____

What contacts do you have? Can you make more?

_____

_____

_____

_____

Now write down:

1) Your financial objectives:

_____

_____

2) Your desired new worth:

_____

3) What is your timeline? How many years of training might you need?

_____

_____

_____

4) How much work experience do you have in the field?

_____

_____

_____

_____

5) Is your goal realistic? Is it possible? What could stop you?

_____

_____

_____

_____

Woody's voice was cutting into my thoughts. "Carl, do you sincerely know what you want, financially?"

"Yes, I do."

"Then I must show you how to rid yourself of your old habits, and how to replace them with better ones. Don't let your old paradigms continue to influence you."

"How can I become optimistic about owning the café, when I don't know what to do next?"

"Become **optimistic** and develop healthy **goal** habits. And have patience with yourself and others. Earl Nightingale once said that your success is the progressive realization of your worthy **goal**."

"What do you mean by worthy?" I asked.

Woody answered, "Any goal that does not violate other people's rights. Now, write down your declared goal, because that is your chief desire."

"Okay." I wrote down 'Own Joe's Café.'

"Now, visualize yourself already owning the cafe."

Visualize yourself already fulfilling your dream. <u>Write about how you think your life would be:</u>

_____

_____

_____

_____

Keep assessing your goals. Are they helping you to go the right direction, to obtain your desires?

Woody was winding up his speech: "Good **goals** guide you on your way in daily life. If you have poorly defined goals, or no *goals*, you will be confused. You could end up going in a circle, and you can drift away from your Divine Purpose. That's why our next lesson, in India, is crucial. It involves **fulfilling** your goals."

"Now Angela and I are going off to enjoy the Bada waterfront and the city. Hope you do the same. Above all, relax. You have already made progress: you have set your **goal**." Woody wrapped his big arm around Angela. "We'll see you back at the hotel tonight. In the meantime, experience the sights and sounds of this busy and productive city! Tomorrow, we depart for New Delhi. Remember, Carl, all completed goals started with the belief that they **can become reality.** Focus on your goal. Nourish it. Sustain it. In India, you will start believing."

That evening, I switched my focus to enjoying the bustling city life, my goal firmly lodged in my subconscious mind. I visited an open-air market area, observed the lively Chinese people, and got jostled and swept along with the night crowd. I smelled the unique mixtures of aromas coming from a vast array of products – many brought in from the countryside. While I observed such a diverse exhibition of goods of every possible kind, I experienced sudden glimpses of serene beauty: two women chatting as their toddlers played, an elderly scholar, reading in a window lit with a golden lamp; a girl laughing with her hand over her mouth as she heard a joke. In my solitude, I became more relaxed. Daydreams filled my mind as I gazed at all the sights.

At dinner time, I stopped at a food stand on crowded Nanjing Road and purchased a half-dozen Shanghai-style dumplings, *gyoza,* from a friendly street vendor. My mind was peacefully guided by Woody's instructions as I continued to leisurely explore this marvelous, crowded city at my own pace.

At last needing some rest, and some attention for my well-used feet, I finally retreated to the Portman Ritz Carlton Hotel, where I enjoyed a relaxing, traditional Chinese massage.

I had seen thousands of hard-working, industrious people, living close together in a city that never slows down. The very thought of tomorrow excited my mind. Feeling physically and emotionally better than I had in months, I happily collapsed onto my soft bed, where I slept like a millionaire.

Stop 3: New Delhi, India... Repeat

I was so hyped up! We had just left the pulsating city of Shanghai behind, and were now flying towards India.

On the way, Woody instructed Joe, his pilot, to fly over the snow-covered Himalayas, the most spectacular natural barrier in the world. From the jet's windows, we also saw alpine valleys, green pine forests, and lonely, flat plains. Then, we flew across the vast, golden wheat fields of northern India.

All the while, the first two words – **"goals"** and **"attitude"** were twisting around in my imagination.

I was writing down my thoughts, testing some new ways to use these first two words. Trying to understand why I couldn't make more money, I tried to link my beliefs to my behavior. As I did so, new, exciting ideas about how to get ownership of Joe's Café began forming in my mind.

Setting aside my notes, I rested in the jet's lounge, reading a travel book about New Delhi and the Taj Mahal. It gave me a taste of what was ahead.

I looked over at Woody and Angela, who were busy going over their wedding plans. I saw how happy they were. It made me miss my wife. I truly wanted a better life for Sally and our children. My mind was beginning to formulate fresh, new ideas to find a way to make that happen.

<u>Think of the ways you can help make a better life, for you and those you love. Write it here:</u>

_____

_____

_____

_____

_____

We flew first to Taj Mahal, instead of New Delhi, landing at Agra's airport. This time, Woody hired a simple form of transport, a local taxi. Our driver, Raj, drive us to the nearby magnificent world wonder, a monumental act of devotion that a powerful husband created in memory of a beloved wife. Soon, we were in awe as we witnessed this colossus monument. The spectacular mausoleum took our breath away. Woody himself was impressed.

"Carl, this monument is incredible, isn't it? Look at its symmetry! Everything is in exact proportion, aligned. Each brick has a twin. And at night, the palace's marble glows."

Woody continued, "Over twenty thousand workers constructed this splendid monument. This shrine started with one brick. Now look at it!

This is a result of tremendous labor, each and every day. Brick by brick. Stone by stone. The goal was set and met. The result is a wonder of the world. This supreme act of love was dreamed, envisioned, and made."

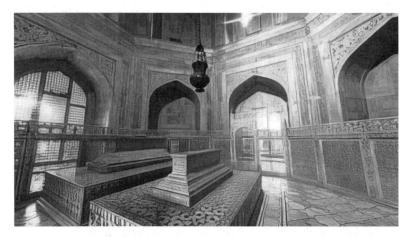

Woody kept drilling into my head that it was all a matter of perseverance, teamwork and resources. A successful day, he said, leads to many successful days. A long enough chain of success creates results, and a life full of success. Repetition and persistence are the driving forces in making that chain.

"Reflect upon your goal you created yesterday, of owning the café," Woody reminded me. "That objective is like the Emperor's dream. He visualized it. Then he made it happen."

"He could have failed," I said. "Run out of money, for example."

"But when you formulate your goal, you begin putting down the bricks for the foundation of your dreams. This process may take a long time, but it ensures that you will realize your goal. It involves the word '**repeat**.' If you fully understand this, you will make it."

"How will I know what to repeat?"

"Because you set smaller goals to reach the bigger ones. Big goals are rarely achieved by accident or without a pre-existing purpose. Mentally **repeat your goals**. Feed your all-powerful subconscious mind with positive thoughts, and it will intuitively guide you to success."

"I still don't understand how to select the right goals to repeat."

"First, you form a goal. Sleep on it and see if it's still on your mind. If it is, it's a goal your powerful sub-conscious mind can believe in. Second, mentally **repeat** that goal. Third, speak it to your emotional mind. Feel it. Live it. Allow your emotional mind to embrace your thinking mind's created goal. Your subconscious, emotional mind will accept your goal, and will generate 'survival ideas' to support it, which it sends to your thinking, intellectual mind. These unique ideas will guide you to a create a concrete reality."

"Maybe," I replied.

"Writing it down helps both your intellect and your sub-conscious to share the information," Woody said. He then carefully wrote:

First, convince your thinking mind that your desired goal is worth the work needed to make it a concrete reality.

Next, your thinking mind must **repeat your goal often** to your emotional mind (sub-conscious) which cannot discern fact from fantasy.

Repetition will convince your emotional mind that your goal is important for survival.

Both kinds of minds then work together to enhance your chances of success.

123

The emotional mind (sub-conscious) intuitively connects to forces in the universe that the thinking mind cannot comprehend or reach. It can connect to the will of God.

It can generate creative, flexible strategies and ideas to protect what it believes already exists, even if it is still only an idea. The thinking mind works only as hard as it thinks it needs to.

To thwart this laziness, take the lead by insisting on **action.** Select the best **ideas** on which to **act**. You may want to ask God for discernment and guidance. You will experience incredible 'luck' if you follow these steps. **Acts** will lead to **results**.

"Carl," Woody said, handing me his written notes, "meditate on what these words mean to you."

Meditate on what these words mean to you. Write them here:

_____

_____

_____

_____

_____

_____

_____

_____

Woody's India Speech

"Thoroughly evaluate the role that each goal plays in completing your master plan ... in this case, it means owning the cafe. Consider how each effort contributes to each other. The thinking mind will understand, but penetrating the emotional mind requires you first internalize these words."

Curious, I asked, "Woody, why does this work?"

"Nobody's perfectly sure. Perhaps, someday science will better explain it. But whenever you **repeat** statements with emotions and a firm belief there are concrete consequences. Some experts describe this phenomenon as auto-suggestion. As I've said before, when you propose ideas to yourself and use visualization with persistence, you will receive an abundant harvest. Know that your personal goals are achievable. Believe that with all your heart. Approach your desires with a magnificent obsession."

"Obsessions are supposed to be dangerous. I've seen advertisements to take drugs to cut off obsessions."

"Don't confuse dedication to your goals with an obsession," Woody countered. "To succeed, you need to cultivate those habits. But even so, many successful inventors and innovators have been labeled 'obsessive' because they often neglected to have balanced lives."

"I agree."

"Even so, you can lead a balanced life and still have a magnificent obsession," Woody replied. "There's a book with that title – *'Magnificent Obsession,'* – by Lloyd C. Douglas. It's one of the inspirational books I've read. A selfish playboy killed a great, kind doctor, whose life was centered on secretly helping people, due to his drunken driving.

That tragedy transformed the playboy from a reckless, worthless lout into a successful, beloved doctor, who also secretly helped a lot of people. The key was that he learned the principle of doing good in secret. It's one of the key principles that will bring you success. Don't tell me why it works. It just does."

"Let your goals drive and dictate your **acts**. Through **repetition** and by ardently **believing**, these goals become reality. Burning desires will be transformed into concrete thoughts and plans that will morph into tangible assets. Eventually, you'll craft your own reality. The ultimate reality of a successful life."

Woody paused, took a deep breath, and added, "Now, write these truths and repeat them whenever you feel discouraged. Then, imagine applying them in different ways."

"This approach makes sense to me."

"Just remember, goal setting is truly only the first step. **Repeating,** while visualizing your goal with intense emotions, fully believing that your goal is already in existence, and **acting** on the ideas your subconscious gives you, will make it happen! By then, you will **already** own the cafe!"

"Carl, it sounds too easy. Why don't more people take this approach? Why do so many people fail to realize their goals?"

"Because people who don't achieve their full potential may hear the message, but they won't work to sow the seeds. 'You reap what you sow!' Attending seminars and buying books can't replace **action.** You must grasp the truth and hold on. By doing so, universal laws can be activated to direct your efforts. Again, what you give out, or sow, you will receive, or reap."

Woody's words were so laced with strange spiritual ideas that it was hard for me to believe them. I had to remind myself how different this man was, now, from what he had once been. That was a miracle in itself.

"Our next stop is New Delhi. An incredible place of many temples, with crowded streets of a different kind from modern Shanghai. Also, of course, hundreds of shrines and palaces."

In India, my senses were overwhelmed. Indeed, this was a land of many contrasts and contradictions. Before now, I might have been overcome by the chaos, noise and traffic everywhere. Yet, throughout that first day, I could sense a spirit of confidence and serenity that abided in the people.

Though the streets were amazingly cramped, with dirty buses cutting corners just a few feet from me, and people shoving baskets in front of my face, trying to sell everything from coconuts to shoe soles, I also saw holy men seated in silent meditation in the very midst of clamor, confusion and congestion. The Indian women, dressed in their colorful sarees, were quite beautiful. Everything was so different from Florida – the excessive heat, the temples and buildings, the swarms of people, the endless rows of shops selling things undreamed-of in the western world. And especially, the smells...

India wielded a powerful assault on the five senses. Its streets were filthy, noisy, packed with people, animals, buses, trucks, cars and carts. The people were amazingly humble. Despite such crowded streets and heavy traffic, I never saw a bad attitude or lack of patience.

Meanwhile, I followed our street tour schedule. I noticed a denim-clad student rubbing the shoulders of a holy man. I watched rows of bullock carts travel alongside the latest luxury cars.

I visited temples full of thousands of statues, saw monkeys revered as gods, viewed weddings and saw funeral pyres where the bodies of the dead were consigned to flames. By sunset in New Delhi, my senses were drained. I was all but trembling from sensory overload.

Finally, after an exhausting and incredible day, at the Imperial Hotel I fell asleep in a clean, comfortable bed. That was a blessing for which I was extremely grateful.

Stop 4: Cape Town, South Africa... Prioritize

As we approached the Dark Continent, Woody instructed his pilot to fly over South Africa's Cape of Good Hope. It was another example of contrasting scenic mountains and cityscapes: I began to realize that many great cities were built with access to the sea for trade, while protected by mountains or deserts from invasions from the interior. Shortly after, Woody's Boeing Business Jet gracefully touched ground at Cape Town's International Airport. As we arrived, I grew excited, contemplating what this great world city might teach me.

"Another beautiful place!" I exclaimed as we stepped foot into the continent of Africa, supposedly the cradle of humanity's birth. After few minutes, Woody's chauffeur, Kuto, arrived, who immediately drove us to the picturesque Victoria and Alfred Waterfront Hotel (our pilot and co-pilot checked in at the Cape Grace Hotel). The area's exciting shops and entertainment centers were intermingled with unique and intriguing business offices.

"When the European settlers first saw this place," Kuto told us from inside the limousine, "they didn't want to leave."

As our limo crawled through the heavy traffic, I observed a colorfully dressed medicine man performing a strange and intoxicating dance. On all sides, I saw rows of world-class hotels and luxurious condominiums surrounding the marina. Getting out of the limo, we began to stroll among the residences and mansions of the very wealthy, soaking up the vibrations of wealth saturating the opulent, cosmopolitan atmosphere. In contrast, we could see a myriad of colorful fishing boats, filled with busy fishermen, departing for Table Bay.

 I couldn't help but say, "This is the most beautiful place I have ever seen!"

"I agree!" Woody replied, his arm around Angela. "Now, Carl, after lunch time, we will take the cable car to Table Bay. From the restaurant patio, we can watch the people pass by. You will once more witness a multitude of many different people from all parts of the world."

As I observed the bustling cosmopolitan environment, Woody continued, "Carl, Cape Town is full of great contrasts. Dr. Christian Barnard performed the world's first heart transplant at Cape Town's Groote Schuur Hospital over fifty years ago, but as you know, behind the façade this town has a dark side."

"I wondered why," I interjected, "you've said nothing negative about any of the cities we've visited."

"Many of the world's nations put up a façade, claiming 'all is well.' Don't believe everything the tour guides say! Dirty politicians, terrorists, organized crime, biased media, drug dealers, prostitution, human trafficking, scammers, pedophiles, smugglers, and pickpockets are just around the corner in most of the world's big cities. As we explore our eight cities, we are deliberately ignoring the wicked, the violent, and the evil. Not because we're ignorant, but because our journey focuses on learning about the honest, the kind, and the good."

With this solemn warning, we ate at Willoughby's, where we enjoyed a tasty **braai**, or barbeque, of chunky, spiced sausage and smoked fish. The spicy meat was followed by a platter of deliciously ripe grapes, melons, peaches, apricots, and plums.

After lunch, we ascended Table Mountain via cable car. As we climbed up toward the mountain's peak, the view below was truly breathtaking. We also saw unique South African plant life of astounding beauty.

It was all preparatory to Woody's next lecture about money.

"Our fourth word, **prioritize,** is a method of determining what is vital in the business of making money, and what is not. It sorts the more profitable actions from the less profitable. The selection process brings you closer and faster to executing your decided goals."

I sensed that this word described my worst problem: handling my time wisely.

"When you **prioritize,** the path to making more money becomes clear. As you prioritize, the cloud of problems and obstacles between you and accumulating money evaporates and is tossed aside."

"Woody, how do I **prioritize?**"

"You develop a priority formula, to get things done in an effective way."

"How?"

"The formula should reflect simplified practical solutions to your current problems. For example, let's look at your goal of owning a cafe. Your immediate task is to clearly define your problem and develop a specialized process towards a solution. Keep focused on your most important common goal."

"How can I do that?" I asked.

"In your notebook," Woody explained, "write down the **eight** most essential tasks you need to do, every day. Do it for tomorrow, just to get started. I assure you that finishing each task, every day, will bring you closer to realizing your goal. Concentrate on what must actually be done to fulfill each of these top eight tasks. Decide which one is the most critical in conjunction to fulfilling your goal. Label it Number One. Do the same for number two, three, et cetera."

Write down the eight most essential tasks you need to do tomorrow, and number them:

_____

_____

_____

_____

_____

_____

_____

_____

Woody paused, and added, "Tomorrow, when you awake, you should immediately begin your efforts to finish 'Number One.' Once completed, you then proceed to number two, and so on. If, by chance, the first task remains incomplete, quickly move on to the second. Do not waste time agonizing, if an uncontrollable delay occurs."

"I'll have to be more flexible, then." I replied. "I tend to work at a task until it's finished – always!"

"Consider the time each step requires. Remember, it's profitable to be flexible concerning each given task. Multi-task, or simultaneously perform more than one task, when possible. If you can perform simultaneous tasks without reducing the quality of each task's outcome, multi-tasking will increase your efficiency."

Write down things that you can easily multi-task (for example, keeping track of your bank balance while paying your bills is a time-saver):

_____

_____

_____

_____

_____

_____

_____

"I could mess up," I feared.

"In some cases, quality can be affected," Woody agreed, "but there are smaller and simpler tasks that can be done together. For example, while you wait for an airplane, you can make short phone calls or review business plans."

"But when do you get a chance to relax, then?"

"Just keep your efforts in a constant forward motion. Remain focused on their necessity, **prioritize** continually, and you will accomplish your stated goals, with time to spare."

"I'll have to change some habits."

"That's right. Start by giving yourself enough time to classify and rank your tasks according to their importance. Postpone unnecessary efforts. The next task on the list can wait if a more crucial task needs to be worked on first. Once you develop the **prioritize** habit and do this every day for a long time, I promise you will notice real progress toward realizing your goal."

"Tell me more," I insisted.

"Maybe this story will motivate you," Woody said.

"A long time ago, there was an efficiency consultant who told a business client to prioritize. He designed a simple, yet elegant plan for his client's employees. The prioritize method added immediate value to his business. Every morning, he was ready to do the most important things that had to do with his business and his goals first. As a result of his success, his client, in gratitude, voluntarily sent him a check equivalent to one million dollars in today's money."

"It's simple enough. I should do it..."

"Yes. But why don't more people try it? Because they get sidetracked into doing less important things.

The **prioritize** method brought the company and its president to the top of their industry because suddenly the company and its people could clearly saw what was imperative for them. They began to ignore all unnecessary tasks."

"Woody, of course, it makes sense," I agreed. "I definitely become less efficient when I get sidetracked."

"When you apply the prioritize principle, you head straight towards your goal."

"I will start applying this tonight," I told him. "I'll write down the eight most important items for tomorrow. In the morning, I'll start with number one and keep going until it's done."

"The method seems so simple, but it's hard to be consistent unless you make it a habit. Remember, we must replace our old bad habits with good new habits."

Attitude – Goals – Repeat – Prioritize

"Since Angela and I will be resting in our suite, and then have to get some work done, use your time alone to reflect on my words. I suggest that you visit the Camps Bay Beach. Then, tomorrow, we will prepare for Europe."

"Okay," I said, my new challenge to prioritize still on my mind. "A South African vender told me to head that way, too. He said that while Camps Bay Beach is one of the world's most beautiful, I shouldn't miss a visit to Robben's Island."

"Remember, Carl, you're here for your own important reasons. On this journey of self-discovery, you are even being isolated from your family. Even Angela and I leave you alone in each city as much as possible. Focus only the positives and avoid the negatives during this personal journey of self-discovery." Woody said.

"But when we get back, I'll have to face all of that," I reminded Woody. "The good, the bad, and the ugly."

"What if you had been unable to get away because of work?" Woody asked. "Luckily, I'm your employer. For those who can't take time off work for this kind of journey, they will need a book to teach and guide them."

A warm feeling flooded over me. "I love to help people. Maybe I will write a book."

"Maybe that's why you were chosen to receive the gold coin!"

My day in Cape Town included a visit to Cape Town's incredible aquarium, where I saw children playing and interacting with all kinds of marine animals big and small. Because it was my birthday, I got in free. I also visited a beach full of cute, rare penguins, only found in this area. A few years earlier, there had been just one breeding pair of this kind of penguin on the beach, but through conservation efforts, now there were thousands!

Grateful for the opportunities I had to learn how to pursue my life goals and dreams, as I took a taxi back to the Cape Grace Hotel, I stayed quiet and thought about writing a book to help others learn what I was learning. The word **prioritize** reminded me that acquiring Joe's Café was my **first priority**. I needed to focus on achieving my biggest dream. It had to take **priority**. "Before I sleep tonight, I need to think about 'the four words' and how to construct my **prioritize** list."

Review 'the four words.' Imagine ways to use them.

_____

_____

_____

That night, I slept soundly, knowing that I had prepared my list for tomorrow. I was determined to make this a life-long habit. I thanked God for guiding me, grateful that Woody entered my life to show me the pathway to financial success.

Stop 5: Berlin, Germany... Think

Flying into Europe from Southern Africa, as we approached Germany's capital, Berlin, from the sky we could see the television tower of Alexander Platz, the Reichstag Building, and the Brandenburg Gate. Only a single, ancient gate to the city remained from the original eighteen. Gazing down, we also saw the eastern part of the city, which had new, beautiful skyscrapers and buildings.

"Carl?" Woody asked, "can you believe this city was completely devastated during the Second World War? Then, for decades, it was divided by a wall. But, now it is united, free, and forward-thinking."

After landing, we arrived at the luxurious Adlon Kempinski Hotel, where Angela planned to relax and enjoy the hotel's luxurious spa. Meanwhile, our German chauffeur, Helmut, was pleased to tell us about Berlin's history as he drove me and Woody in a red Mercedes along the city's spectacular boulevard, Unter den Linden, to the Brandenburg Gate. There, we exited the car and looked upon the splendid gate, with its bronze horses and chariots at its summit.

"It is amazing to stand here," I thought. "What an experience this trip has been! Seeing so many new sights and learning so much about how other people live in Asia, Africa and Europe!"

Earlier, I'd fantasized about these places in travel books, but now they had become part of my reality. As we took the walkway to the Brandenburg Gate, Woody explained, "During the Cold War, the Brandenburg Gate symbolized the division between East and West Berlin. In 1989, soon after Hungary began to let their people escape to freedom, Berlin followed suit, and the great Wall between the two German countries was broken open. Today, this Gate symbolizes German reunification."

As Woody and I entered the building, Woody said softly, "Let us go into the 'Room of Silence,' where I will tell you about the fifth word, **think**."

As we approached the Room of Silence, Woody, in a surprisingly reverent voice, whispered, "Carl, this is where the 'weary and frenzied' can sit and meditate. Sometimes, our minds need silence, and time to **think**. Here, consider how you use your incredible mind machine.... For most people, the best time to **think** is usually in the morning, when the world seems silent and at peace. Unless, of course, it's someone like you who must hurry to work. For that reason, you might prefer to set aside an hour to **think** at night."

As we sat there, in silence, we were not alone. There were dozens of other visitors, whose clothing and faces showed that they had come here from many countries.

As we stood up again from the bench, Woody said softly, "**Think**, plan, and research your ambitions. I challenge you to commit to spending an hour every day – or night – to **think**. These hours will become precious brainstorming sessions for you. Setting aside this time will produce your most creative thinking. You can also allocate this time to read and acquire new information in your areas of interest."

What hour can you reserve to dedicate to thinking?

_____ Set this hour aside each day.

Woody's Berlin Speech

"Each day, focus your mind on what is critical and refocus how you plan to accomplish your goals. Through proper planning and meditation, ideas are transformed into achievements. This technique allows your emotional mind to communicate with you. Each morning, or at the best time for you, write your main goal. You can also use this selected hour to update your strategies, such as writing down supporting ideas that will help achieve your primary goal."

"I've never even thought of doing anything like this."

"Remember, *one* good idea can sufficiently change your life and your business. Your mind is invaluable! Though we use only a fraction of its capacity, we must make a daily effort to harness our subconscious mind's potential. Make it work for you! Allow its unique ideas to lead you toward accomplishing and achieving your goals."

As we walked around the corner of Brandenburg Gate, we stopped to gaze at the oldest part of the stone wall, where I spotted a bit of paper that had been pushed inside a crack. When I pulled out the small scrap of paper, imagine my astonishment to find just one word written on it: "**Think.**"

Was this the beginning of the miracles I was told to expect?

I was still standing there, stunned, when Woody announced, "Carl, I must return to our hotel for a business meeting. I suggest that you visit the Wall Museum and the other nearby sites. Take your time. You'll have the whole day, tonight, and most of tomorrow, to explore and **think.** Then, we will depart for Paris."

After Woody left, as I strolled through a museum of art, I remembered that Woody, being a billionaire, had acquired the hotel's incredible Brandenburg Gate Suite for himself and Angela, which featured a breathtaking view of the ultramodern concert hall that housed the Berlin Philharmonic Symphony. Luckily, from a Turkish street scalper I acquired a last-minute ticket. Inside the vast music hall, I enjoyed the marvelous acoustics that were created under the huge, suspended sound boards, bringing Europe's best classical music resonating into my soul.

Stop 6: Paris, France... Serve

We only stayed one day in Berlin. As Woody's private jet approached Paris, the fresh morning sun had just broken through the cloudy horizon.

Slowly from the air, as the dark land received a fresh coating of morning sunlight, we were able to see traces of France's premier city before we landed.

Gazing down at the morning skyline, Woody explained, "Carl, Paris is often called 'the world's most beautiful city' or 'the City of Lights.' Its monuments and national treasures are better preserved here than in almost any other world city. Even in my darkest hours, Paris and its romance always gave me hope that life could be fulfilling."

As the sunlight increased, Woody ordered Joe, our pilot, to deliberately fly over the stunning palace of Versailles.

"I obtained a permit to do that," he said, smiling. As we soared above King Louis XIV's sprawling estate, I could see its magnificent gardens and majestic buildings in a layout that could only be seen in the movies.

Around 7AM

When Woody's Business Jet touched ground at Paris's Charles de Gaulle International Airport, and since part of Woody's business was in Paris, he was immediately greeted by a group of his French colleagues.

After a short meeting where they reviewed some paperwork, Woody, Angela and I took a limousine to his favorite hotel near the Seine River's stone-lined banks.

After checking in, Woody insisted that he relax alone with Angela at the luxurious spa. They had seen all the sights in Paris numerous times, and, as Woody had already explained, I was supposed to be on my own, to **think,** as much as possible.

Alone and absorbed in thought, I stopped to visit a bakery, allured by the pastries I saw in the window. Full of the kind of curiosity only a restaurant manager might have, I bought one of each kind to taste. "I'd love to bring French pastries like these into Joe's Café!" I told myself. Paris was inspiring me to think about what improvements I could make to ensure the café's success. Next, I visited a fine restaurant and ordered a typical French breakfast. As I tasted my chocolate-laced croissant, sipped café au lait, and tried to read a French newspaper, I found myself returning to Woody's words:

Prioritize! – Think!

I set aside the newspaper, took out a pen and began writing...

Later that morning, Woody greeted me in the marble-floored lobby, appearing rejuvenated. He asked, "Did you enjoy your breakfast?"

"French food is incredible, especially the pastries and the bread!"

"Have you meditated over the five words? And what they mean to you?"

"I almost can't quit thinking about them."

"When you are ready, they will become part of you, like a reflex. You will find yourself almost unconsciously thinking about them. They will finally become familiar and habitual to your subconscious mind. Then spontaneous inspirations will lead your readied mind to new insights and ideas."

Minutes later, Woody changed the subject. Would I like a special tour of the city? We soon left the hotel and were quickly taken to that famous and enormous iron structure, the Eiffel Tower, where Woody proceeded to give me another lecture.

"Carl, see this magnificent tower? In 1889, Mr. Eiffel constructed this world symbol. What was once a World Fair exhibit is now a permanent icon for Paris, for France, and for the World! Let's go to the top!"

Woody had arranged for us to enter a private elevator that would take us to the highest level of the Tower, where our tour guide presented us a panoramic view of Paris below.

She was an extremely friendly, service-oriented woman, skilled in passionately describing Paris' key points of interest.

She knew everything about its landmarks, its finest shops, its most remarkable buildings. As she spoke with her sweet, soft voice, I couldn't help but feel her positive vibrations as she effortlessly shared her high enthusiasm for her city, her country, and her culture.

"I can't believe how much she loves this city!" I told myself, impressed by her enthusiasm. In all that she described, our guide presented each facet of her home city in a very positive light. She was serving her clients well by loving what she did. Surely, she was fulfilling a Divine Purpose by so thoroughly entertaining the tourists of Paris.

After our tour, we enjoyed a classic French lunch. As we ate, I remarked to Woody, "This delicious food is making me think about how to turn Joe's Café into a first-class establishment. And speaking of first class, wasn't our tour guide's attitude refreshing?"

"Yes. She's an example of our next word, **serve.** Carl, since you worked so many hours at the café, you, of all people, know what it means to **serve** others."

"It's easy, when you give from your heart," I reflected, thinking about my old job. "I was sincere and was pretty positive."

"Yes, if you **serve,**" Woody agreed, between sips of coffee. "It was the biggest lesson I had to learn, and I learned it from you! To **serve** is not only crucial for today, but also for tomorrow. I learned from you that we should always try to go the extra mile in all our efforts. When you channel your energies into **serving** others, you will eventually receive an abundant harvest. For when you give out good, good comes back."

"I saw that at my café," I recalled. "At the café, my customers genuinely needed me to **serve** them, with my full attention."

"Yes," Woody agreed, "I saw how you focused on serving others quite well. But often, when you served others, did you know you were actually serving yourself?"

"I never noticed any of that," I told him.

"It's because of how you served me, without resentment, that inspired me to hire you."

I thought, 'When you give much of yourself, people will also give much back to you.' "But how can I do any of that in my life today?" I asked.

"I've thought about that," Woody replied. "For your current situation, you need to analyze how you can be of service to others now. I suggest that you list eight categories of people that you feel you **must serve.** In this process, push aside your own short-term needs. Forget your immediate desires. That extra mile that you walk today will ensure that you will realize your goals, which includes earning more money!"

"Well, since I intend to own a business, I would say my customers are one category."

"Good! Name seven others."

After a pause, I added, "Employees, employers, prospects, neighbors, associates, families, and friends."

"Very good, Carl! Now, for each situation you encounter in your business, running a cafe, consider how you can improve service relations. How can you best **serve** and help others? For example, how can you improve service for **future** customers? How can you best serve them?"

After I gave Woody a few answers, he continued, **"Next,** imagine eight ways to **serve** each category. As you make a habit of thinking **how** to serve, what happens when you do this – preferably every day – will lead to some pleasing outcomes.

Also, before you begin any other tasks, consider how you can better serve others on this particular day. Allocate more time to serve when you are feeling fresh. Usually in the morning."

145

"At the café, I intuitively served people."

"Yes, what started as a deliberate act, eventually was transformed into a habitual response. But, your rewards are always in relationship to the value of what you can do. Wages reflect the value of your service to society. For example, sports stars are highly paid because they entertain so many. Many millions of people willingly pay a lot to watch sports."

"True," I agreed.

"The key is to treat everybody as VIPs. Say to yourself, 'I will make a good impression and serve this person.' Pretend that this is your last chance to make a great impression. Remember, you will reap tremendous rewards when you serve everyone as well as you can. It is a universal law. A law of attraction. You will eventually attract those who will want to give you exactly what you seek."

List eight categories of people that you feel you must serve. In this process, push aside your own short-term needs:

_____

_____

_____

_____

_____

_____

Later, after Woody again encouraged me to go for a walk, I explored Paris's cobblestoned streets. I saw souvenir shops, more bakeries, butcher shops, flower carts, cafes, bars, and the chic boutiques adored by fashion-conscious Parisian women. I heard people greet each other with "bonjour!"

Many of these people seemingly soaked up life, basking in their culture and in their enjoyment of everyday living. I watched the flowing Seine River, observed the curve of its stretched-over bridges and the ornate stone buildings along both sides.

I devoted more than one **"think"** hour to visit The Louvre, where I pondered The Mona Lisa and felt the impact of many masterpieces on my soul. As I left The Louvre and began walking along the tree-lined boulevards, I admired Paris for being such a carefully planned city. This city was made for people! I imagined the word **serve** as I viewed the great variety of people conducting business with each other.

When I stopped to view the famous statue by Rodin, "**The Thinker**," I said to myself, "**Think** is the word that inspired this masterful work of art," and my mind momentarily flashed back to Berlin.

Although this was only my second European experience, I felt surrounded by a deep sense of history, especially when contemplating the value and meaning of human civilization, music, and the arts. I considered how, in many ways, "Life is art in Paris, and art is life."

The city's every detail reflected a true stamp of human achievement. Reinvigorated and inspired, that evening I

147

happily dined with Woody and Angela at Le Jules Verne, inside The Eiffel Tower.

Stop 7: London, Great Britain… Honesty

As we approached our next European stop, London, in our jet plane, Woody excitedly pointed down at a huge, glittering Ferris Wheel. "Look! There's The London Eye!"

After we landed, Angela was met by one of her best friends, who whisked her way for the day. Skipping breakfast, we began our London sight-seeing on one of the "Hop-on, Hop off" buses.

London was full of "corner pubs" and ethnic restaurants based on the many cuisines of the former British colonies. Bedecked with sprawling parks, stone churches, and small, peaceful squares surrounded by boutique hotels and shops, the busy streets were crammed with life and color.

Next, we rode along Oxford Street, which seemed filled end-to-end with bright buses and white, black and yellow taxis.

There were foreign tourists of many races and colors mingling with the wide variety of Londoners, who were also of many races and colors. Above all, I was endlessly fascinated with London's famous landmarks and unique attractions.

We visited The Tower of London, where we viewed the Royal Crown Jewels, witnessed The Changing of the Guard at St. James Place, and explored Madame Tussaud's famous Wax Museum. After a visit to Sherlock Holmes' apartment full of mysteries, we finally took a taxi to The London Eye.

After a thrilling ride on The Eye, where we could view The London Bridge, Big Ben and Buckingham Palace, we climbed aboard a final bus to see Buckingham Palace and Big Ben up close. Our very informative tour guide charmed us with her typical strong English accent and sweet voice.

Soon, the world's most famous clock, Big Ben, came into view. "You're in luck, people," she said. "Big Ben's bells are about to ring!" Suddenly, Big Ben's bells began to chime: it was 4 PM. As the bells reverberated into silence, our tour guide said, "Big Ben has kept exact time for the nation since 1859. When you hear it ringing, you can almost feel its place in history. The distance between Buckingham Palace, our next destination, and Big Ben is only 4176 feet."

Our tour guide continued to give us an incredible amount of information. She was not only a friendly Londoner, she had trained herself to be a walking, talking history book and statistician. She knew all the city's facts, factoids and legends.

"That tour guide gave us a thrilling experience!" I told Woody, as we left the bus.

"I was impressed, too!" Woody exclaimed, as we turned our gaze upon the Thames River. "She had so information to share. And because of how friendly and knowledgeable she was, we trusted her statements and benefited from them. When you conduct yourself with integrity, you'll find that people will tend to trust and respect you."

The Power of the Mind

"You can have all the information in the world," Woody reminded me, "but without the emotional sub-conscious part of your mind, you won't have access to the creative ideas you need to make good use of that information. Repeating the ideas that come into your mind," Woody said, "and writing them down so they won't be lost, and being fully receptive to positive thoughts, as I've told you, will strengthen your emotional mind, which cannot distinguish between fantasy, beliefs, and reality. Remember, it accepts what you choose to feed it."

"Use your creative energy to harness your plans into action, and good results will fall into place," he said.

"Your thinking and emotional mind must learn to function together harmoniously, just as Big Ben's clockwork and bells, which are so different from each other, work so well together. When they are synchronized, they manifest clear results. Whenever imaginative impulses pop into your thinking mind, before you lose them, **write them down!** Then put them to use. **Truth** is the most crucial word, because it will correctly link our acts together into a logical, harmonious chain. Without integrity, trust can be lost, your chain of logic and inspiration will break apart, and you can lose your way."

"Right now," I said, "I want to use my creative energy to find a good restaurant. I'm famished!"

We stopped to eat at an Irish pub, where we were served foaming pints of Guinness, authentic Irish stew, and big slabs of bread and butter. After enjoying an hour of live Irish music and dancing, it was time to take a taxi back to the hotel. Angela had not yet returned: as we waited for her in the lounge, Woody decided to resume his lecture.

Goals – Repeat – Ideas – Action – Reality

"If my positive thoughts are so important for the emotional mind," I queried, "Am I never supposed to allow myself to think negative thoughts?"

Woody explained that if you construct a positive mental filter that can harness the emotional mind, which is significantly more powerful than the thinking mind, you will have control over your emotions when negative thoughts and events occur.

"When you channel positive thoughts," he said, "those thoughts relate to fulfilling your goal. You can guide your emotional mind's full strength to deal with that task. Your positive, emotional thoughts and impulses will strengthen, involving love, friendship, creation, enthusiasm, hope, and faith."

"How will I know it's happening?" I asked.

"Well, Carl, you can feel it happening," Woody reflected. "Your mind completes your goal first. Once you conquer the mental battle, your intellectual thoughts will flow towards your lower brain and elevate your capacity to feel, to love and to serve. In a matter of time, **You will become what you think.** I know, because it happened to me!"

"Yes. I *can* ... **become what I think,**" I agreed, beginning to visualize how I would pursue my long-term planning.

"Our mind is incredibly complex; yet we only tap into a fraction of it. Today, Carl, our topic includes **honesty,** the most important and fundamental word of them all. People live and die for what they believe to be the truth. Make **honesty** your firm foundation, at all costs."

"What do you mean?" I protested. "Above all, I *am* honest."

"Don't take offense, Carl. Let me explain. Remember Big Ben? Big Ben always tells us the time, but only if it's kept in good repair can we trust it. Just as you must do, concerning protecting your core of integrity. I'm not talking about harmless white lies that help us get along with each other. I'm talking about being faithful to your **inner truth**. You must be truthful to yourself."

"Inner truth?" (To me, there was only one kind of truth).

"Carl, it is your true character, your loyalty, your integrity, your set of core ideas, which you must never betray. Ask yourself often, 'Is it the truth?' Also, listen to your inner voice that seeks the truth. Use 'I will do my best' as a slogan." You must repeat such slogans to yourself."

"And then, what?"

"Do your best."

"I always try," I told him.

"You will know because your intuition will guide you. Always pursue *honesty*. Even when it may be painful to face certain facts about yourself or others, you must protect the truth from being twisted. How you handle your inner truth is the pivotal connection between your intellectual mind and your emotional mind."

"I always felt uncomfortable even taking a dollar I found on the floor, at the café," I told Woody.

"It is that core of integrity that can help guide you," Woody answered. "It was one of the hardest lessons I learned these past three years. I had to correctly discern what was good as well as true, instead of just going after what I wanted. Become sensitive to your intuitive feelings," Woody urged me. "Imbalances occur if your intellect insists on conflicting with your intuition. If events occur differently than hoped, remaining frank and upfront with yourself will cultivate a harmonious relationship between your thoughts and actions."

I understood this matter well: every time I acted against my "gut feelings" I regretted ignoring them.

"I'll give you an example of what I mean," Woody said. "Such as, if someone spreads lies about your best friend. If you remain silent and allow the lies to spread, you practice a form of dishonesty. If you witness wrong actions, speak out. If you take these risks, over time, you be respected for your integrity."

"That got me fired, once."

"Have you heard the expression that says, 'the truth will set you free' or 'the truth is all powerful'? Follow what you know is true. For you, stealing a penny is a crime. But there are others who can't see what you see. Let them learn from you how valuable it is to work with someone who is always honest and truthful. I had to learn how to exhibit polite and kind behavior, Carl, even when I didn't want to. As I did so, I began to value others who treated me the same. Eventually, I also had to admit that the truth always wins, in the end. Defend the truth when it's in danger, and your heart and mind will find purpose and peace, knowing your life has been worthwhile. When you connect with those you love, and with those who love you, you have opportunities to practice it and be strengthened by its simplicity."

Woody responded to my open admiration of London's stimulating blend of old and new buildings and the tranquility of its spaces when he said, "This city uniquely represents a combination of tradition and modernity. And it works. In the same way, our intellectual mind and our emotional mind will get along, if we stay honest to ourselves."

Woody frowned. "I remember how I'd blow up at people, and then get drunk, telling myself I needed the comfort of alcohol to face the problems in my miserable life. I was telling myself a batch of lies. One more thing," Woody said. "Our time is limited. We only possess a limited amount of time, so effective use of it is a top priority. Combine your honest efforts and your effective use of time with the powers of your mind, and you become unbeatable."

<u>Write down each activity you did yesterday:</u>

_____

_____

_____

_____

Then estimate how well you think you used your time:

_____

_____

_____

_____

_____

What did you accomplish that day?

_____

_____

_____

_____

Did your actions get you closer to your goal?

_____

_____

_____

_____

_____

"Carl, I have some business to take care of, but you still have some time to explore more of this marvelous city tonight and tomorrow morning, before we cross the Atlantic. I want you to visit Trafalgar Square, Piccadilly, the British Museum, and the National Gallery."

"I can't believe how much this trip has expanded my mind."

"You're being exposed to different lifestyles and cultures," Woody commented. "As you learn what each lifestyle has to offer, you will be better able to **serve**, and success will materialize," he assured me. "Just as I discovered balance, you, too, will obtain the income you desire, once you master these words and these habits. They will help you grow character, integrity, and inner honesty. When you learn ways to emotionally connect with each word, they produce results."

Woody's London Speech

"If you only touch the surface of these words and only casually react to them, you will gain the necessary insight to use them to change your life," he told me.

Woody had to attend a business reception with Angela at the London Hilton, so as soon as she arrived, they departed, leaving me alone to savor the rest of the evening and what it had to offer.

First, I took the London Underground to Piccadilly Circus, where I sat in The Tube with transients, polished professionals, students, tourists and common workers, all trying to get home. I even caught a glimpse of a lawyer wearing his 18th century wig and gown. After strolling through Piccadilly Circus' exclusive underground shops, I got on The Tube again. Five minutes

157

later, I reached The Embankment Station at the river, where I caught a Thames Clipper ferry.

As we crossed The Thames, several lit-up riverboats passed by, full of partying passengers. Lights sparkled their reflections from illuminated bridges sparkled their reflections into the river. The Parliament Building glowed, swathed in golden light. Rising on the other side of The Thames, The Globe Theatre seemed a ghostly visitor from the past, capped by the only thatched roof in all of London. Its big porch facing the river was crowded with well-dressed people enjoying refreshments in the twilight.

Thanks to some cash Woody handed me, I was able to get a box seat at The Globe, one of the few that wasn't sold out, to watch Shakespeare's *Much Ado About Nothing.*

Inside, I was plunged into the world of the 1600's. When I looked up, I could see the sky. After the play, which I enjoyed thoroughly, was over, and this beautiful night came to an end, I thought to myself, "What a wonderful world!"

Stop 8: Rio De Janeiro, Brazil... Gratitude

Despite my best intentions, I overslept. That afternoon, as I boarded Woody's jet, I promised myself that someday I'd be back, with my wife at my side.

We flew into the vibrant city of Rio: it would be our last stop. By then, I realized that it was all up to me, if I was going to be successful. From the air, once again, I observed a huge city, sprawled out against sky and mountains. Yet each city I'd entered had rendered its own unique character, charm, culture, and secrets.

Woody said, "What an enormous city Rio is! Look how tightly it is squeezed between the mountains and the sea. Look at the Copacabana Beach, over there. It's crammed with people swimming, playing soccer, jogging, and sunbathing!

But my mind was elsewhere, contemplating the fact that if changes were to happen, I had to seize the initiative.

I had waited for the Divine Voice, had hoped that Woody, or my neighbors, friends, family, or community would step forward to help me, when it was my own actions that were needed to achieve financial success! I alone was responsible for the outcome. I had to take the initiative and press to win.

After checking in at the Marina All Suites Hotel, where a Samba orchestra played tantalizing music as we enjoyed a quick lunch, Woody tried to raise my spirits by taking me on a trip to the Cocovado Mountain in a twenty-minute cog train ride through the rain forest.

The view from the mountain peak provided a spectacular panorama of Rio and its surroundings. We also marveled at the statue, "Christ the Redeemer," one of the world's greatest landmarks. Woody was clearly impressed with the statue and its message of hope.

"Carl, from nearly every part of the city, this brightly lit statue is visible. It's even seen by all the poor, living down there in their cardboard shacks. We have a great view of everything from up here, don't we?"

"I wish I had a better mobile phone," I told him. "My photos for Sally don't show half of the amazing sights I'm viewing."

"Carl, we have now arrived at our last stop. First, I want you to honestly tell me if you completely understand the purpose and use of all the seven words you've been given, so far?"

"What do you mean?" I asked. "Of course, I do."

"I mean, do you not only understand them intellectually, but are you using your feelings, to deal with them?"

"I think so. I've done a hell of a lot of writing."

"Intellectually, you have probably understood the message of the seven words. But if you are simply agreeing with me and saying, 'I believe that is true,' how do I know you're using your gut instincts, that you're truthfully feeling the power of those words, deep inside?"

"If you mean, how can I emotionally comprehend the seven words, I guess I have to just keep trying."

"I had to learn to **live** them," Woody said. "And that translated into a new life for me! You must access their ability to change

160

your life, so you can financially prosper, like I do. Great principles are only good when applied. If they sit on a shelf or remain unutilized, their potential is irrelevant. I know you're feeling overwhelmed," he added. "Do you remember when you first handed me the gold coin, with the eight values on it and the action words? **Love, serve, create, enjoy**?"

"Yes. How can I forget?"

"At first, I didn't pay much attention to those words. But shortly after, very strange stuff started to happen. When I touched that special coin, within me I felt a surge of energy – a special power. And I found myself reading the inscription over and over. Those eight words: **Attitude – Goals – Repeat – Prioritize – Think – Serve – Honesty - Gratitude**.

"Here's another gold coin, Carl," Woody said, reaching into his left pocket. "I cast it, especially for you." Woody opened his hand, revealing a golden coin. Its inscription held the same Eight Magic Words: **Attitude – Goals - Repeat – Prioritize – Think – Serve – Honesty – Gratitude.** I hope, by now," he said, "that you truly want to grasp the message." When Woody placed the coin in my hand, I grasped it tightly. I want you to take it, to remind you, always, of those eight key words. Keep it on you all the time. Look at it as often as you can. And apply those words to your life."

With awe and admiration, I admired the gold coin, which was identical to the magical coin I'd handed over to Woody."I am forever grateful that you taught me this wisdom,"

Woody said, looking up at the huge Christ statue, with its outstretched arms, so visible on the mountain top, "Carl, you only have to believe! Believe in what God has designed you to do. I hope you find an inner peace. That you set aside your worries. Believe in yourself! Develop a conscious gratitude for what you can do, not only for yourself, but for God, country, community, family and friends."

"I wonder if I can stand so tall," I mumbled.

"Strive to maintain a positive state of mind. Keep your goals alive by planning your moves every day, repeating your goals every day. **Repeat!** Set aside time for constructive thinking. Allocate time to think. Maintain honesty with yourself and others. Treat everyone you meet with kindness, respect and dignity. Surround yourself with inspiring people."

Woody was a living example of what a man with many personal problems could become, following those very words.

"I want you to enjoy Copacabana Beach," he said. "Let's go."

"We're going to another beach? But why?"

As we arrived at the enormous beach, Woody commented, "Did you know that Copacabana is the site of the world's biggest party?

Every New Year's eve, the world's biggest party occurs right on this beach. Bigger than Times Square. Bigger than anywhere. Yes, there were fireworks, but fireworks are everywhere at New Year's. Nobody knows how the world's biggest party came to be. It just did."

"Only a beach the size of this one could hold so many people. Lucky they have such a huge beach," I said.

"There was nothing 'lucky' about it," Woody replied. "This beach is 90% the work of human hands. The result of human needs, human dreams, and human determination. It's the same for you. Hold onto your dreams, do the work, and your dreams will come true."

I spent my final, precious hours at Copacabana Beach, which was a microcosm of Brazilian life, alone. It was a parade of tanned bodies in constant motion. I saw everything from dog walkers, to surfers carrying their boards, to laughing, bronzed cariocas in the tiniest of bikinis. Volleyball games, barefoot venders selling guarana soft drinks and Cervejo beer, businessmen with briefcases making deals, and

Musclemen bobbing up and down on the chin-up bars competed for my attention with roller bladders, joggers, and cyclists cruising by.

I ended the evening dining in a huge Brazilian barbecue involving dozens of kinds of delicious meats.

After a full day in Rio, I was totally exhausted, so I slept well, even with Woody's final messages churning around in my mind.

The next day, we were back home. When we arrived in Tampa, my family was there to meet us at the landing strip. It was a very emotional moment. I'd only been in contact with Sally's voice, and a tiny glass screen showing her face as we'd talked: to see her in the flesh, so healthy and so happy, gave me a surge of joy that no amount of money could match. My wife could see how much my attitude had changed. As I greeted our children, I repeated to myself, *Life was good! So very good!*

The following afternoon, according to Woody's plan, we enjoyed a "Welcome Back Party" and dinner at a restaurant on Bayshore Boulevard. After dinner, as we all walked along Bayshore Boulevard's beautiful bay front, my son, standing close by the water, pointed at something in the water.

"Dad!" he exclaimed. "Look!"

A dark object was protruding from the calm surface, of the water, half-buried in the sand.

I immediately approached the water's edge to get a closer look. It was a dark glass object, deeply etched by time...

Reaching down, I pried the object free and held it high so my son could see that it was a decorative, very ancient bottle.

It was a black onion-shaped glass with a long stem. The sealed bottle carried an inscription in cursive that faintly read, *"IS 1693."* I nervously showed it to Woody, who asked me to carefully unplug its well-worn cork. "You know I have such thick fingers," he said. "You'll have to do it."

Inside was a yellowed scroll.

With trembling hands, I struggled to shake the bottle, trying to remove the rolled-up paper from the narrow opening. Finally, I managed to tighten up the scroll and pull it from the bottle. As I carefully unrolled the scroll, I couldn't believe what I was reading: **it was the deed for Joe's Café!**

"My 'thank you' for helping me so much this year," Woody told me. "Your intervention in my life helped me make another billion dollars! I worried that the bottle might drift out to sea, so I had it watched. And they anchored it for me pretty deep. This is your chance, Carl!"

"I can't take this!" I objected.

"You have to," Woody replied. "I've eaten so much fantastic food on our trip that I'm ashamed to own a place like Joe's Café. Maybe you'd be able to make it into a world-class establishment. I sure as hell would like to see you try."

PART III:
THE WAY &
THE TECHNIQUE

In life, there are four "*individual*" values and four "*relationship*" values. When you can clearly recognize, define and visualize your ideals, you will succeed. Success is the progressive realization of worthy ideals.

(1) Familiarize yourself with the eight life values.

(2) Take time; explore your inner values.

(3) Reflect upon each value's role in your life; project a favorable image for each value.

(4) Place positive ideas into your subconscious mind; visually frame them in your mind.

(5) Ignite your feelings, associate positive outcomes with each goal. Refine the process into a life changing experience.

(6) Maintain a positive outlook; form a clear picture of success.

(7) Be grateful for your accomplishments; what you have.

(8) Celebrate your success and your loved one's successes.

Since only *you* should define your personal goals, do not fear criticism from others.

These are your first few steps in the lifelong journey toward creating and maintaining a winning formula to achieve your dreams.

First, a review. Let's identify our prescribed individual values:

BODY: your physical health

MIND: your mental health

WORK: your labor & career

MONEY: your income & wealth

Begin by grading each life value, using a scale of 1 to 5.

1 = **poor**

2 = **fair**

3 = **good**

4 = **very good**

5 = **excellent**

What is your current status, in a few words? Be honest with yourself.

Remember, when you inspect your life and ask yourself these questions, only you can determine your own evaluation.

Let's start with your first individual value: the body. Our body is an incredible machine that keeps going and going. Despite some abuse and illness, it is amazingly resilient.

We should be very thankful that our fantastic body works so well.

Next, examine yourself and ask: "How would you like to improve your physique?" Your goal could be to simply feel and look better; maybe you would like to create good habits? As an individual, you are unique and only you should decide your physical goals. Remember that no matter what your goals are, or how limited they might be by a damaged body, continue holding onto optimistic thoughts. They will help generate more happiness and peace of mind. Stability is best found with consistency. So, how can we improve ourselves using the first value? Here are some examples of body slogans.

Possible "Body" Slogans:

1. "I will briskly walk 20 minutes a day."

2. "My body is terrific."

3. "I am losing weight."

4. "I am smoke-free."

5. "I am healthy."

6. "Every day, I am getting slimmer and slimmer."

7. "I always eat with moderation."

8. "I will get better and feel better."

Memorize slogans you can identify with or create new slogans that will best work for you.

169

Write Your "Body" Slogans:

_____

_____

_____

_____

_____

_____

After you create your goals:

1) **Repeat positive slogans that will best inspire you.**
2) **Imagine having already obtained your goal.**
3) **Develop a strong consistent feeling of accomplishment.**

Having mentally fulfilled it, you can then "fool" or redirect your subconscious or deeper mind into believing that your ideas are true. Once you convince your subconscious mind that it is real, it will cooperate with your intellectual understandings to help you realize your goals. Sudden thoughts of inspiration will occur more frequently: it is up to you to decide how to act upon these ideas that seem to come from nowhere.

Remember that these inspirational messages and ideas will be coming to you through your subconscious mind. As it communicates with you, your subconscious mind can lead you forward in your pursuit of happiness. By maintaining a positive outlook, you can better harness this very powerful tool...your subconscious mind.

Your brain collects instructions, positive or negative, from your conscious thoughts. It can be likened to a giant reservoir that feeds you with thoughts and ideas directly in conjunction to your situation.

Think about your conscious mind as your personal computer, at home or at work. Your subconscious mind acts like the Internet, providing you with an unlimited source of information. If you can identify your burning desires, you can channel your internal "Internet" to meet your goals.

Internet sites, like inspirational thoughts, provide you with the ideas. For example, your idea can act as a small seed that can blossom into reality and become a full-grown oak tree. If you can visualize the full-grown oak tree, your subconscious mind will provide you with the nourishing sources – water, sunshine, soil and air – so you can reach your strong desire, the full-grown oak tree.

Your subconscious mind will guide and nudge you along towards a specific destination.

Your subconscious mind can function like an automobile and a map, essential tools for your life journey. However, you first must determine how to create your future. Projecting, planning and taking action is the whole essence of how you can accomplish your goals. The extremely powerful subconscious mind can be directed in ways to assist you on your journey.

Often it can behave in inexplicable, yet incredible ways that will sometimes seem to automatically grant you favorable results. Try it!

View yourself as a winner, an achiever. Seize those positive signals to fuel your mind to reach its destination. When you see yourself already there, you feed your subconscious mind with signals. The rest is the incredible work of your subconscious mind.

Possible "Body" Slogans:

"I will eat more healthy food"

"I will exercise more"

"I am losing weight"

"I am aware of what I put in my mouth"

"I do not smoke"

Only **you** should identify your personal goals. Repeat your chosen slogan with intense feeling and focus. Consciously keep yourself into the **"FOA"** mode (Feeling of Accomplishment!).

By concentrating your mental energy on the reality you want, your subconscious mind will respond to support it, because it cannot not distinguish a fantasy (dream, goal, wish, and belief) from a reality. Act upon your images of reality as if they have already materialized. Dreams do come true when you utilize your imagination. We were gifted with imaginations for a reason. We can prepare for the future. Believe your images of the future to be tangible! Continual repetition will generate more positive signals and will build stronger faith in your images of the future. This method could be described as self-suggestion, self-hypnosis or autosuggestion. Don't isolate your dreams from others. We are also here to help each other!

When your subconscious mind registers your fantasies (dreams, goals, wishes, beliefs) into realities, it acts in the most efficient ways possible.

After applying your slogans consistently over time, your fantasies will materialize. Flashes of inspirational thoughts or hunches will appear. These intuitive thoughts will influence you in how to achieve your desires. Whenever you receive the inspirational thoughts from your subconscious mind, it is critical to take immediate action.

Once you formulate your set of goals, you need to write them down on a paper or in the allocated space provided, to help you memorize your dreams. Next, start to act upon this dream with passionate mental repetition. Apply these slogans to your conscious mind several times each day:

1) Just before you step out of bed in the morning

2) At mid-morning

3) At mid-afternoon

4) Just before you fall asleep at night

Practice this vigorously and soon, amazing things will start to happen. Continually meditate about how you can enhance each value. Repeat your thoughts with intense feelings and focus, imaging that you have already accomplished your goals. Be receptive to your inner thoughts and reflect upon them. Your mind was designed for you to recognize these special messages so with focus you can recognize these signals that were meant for you and your pursuit of happiness.

After you have constructed your first "body" value, you can proceed with your second value, your "mind". Find ways to generate positive, optimistic thoughts about your surroundings and yourself.

What methods can you use to positively alter your thought patterns? The repetition of positive slogans will slowly sink and absorb into your subconscious mind. Your attitude will change. Apply a different slogan for your mind. For example, say to yourself: "I feel great. I feel fantastic. I feel terrific." Soon you will start feeling as you are thinking. Don't be discouraged if you do not feel better right away. You need to repeat these slogans over and over sustaining a belief that they are true. You will soon discover that people around you will start noticing your transformation. Your appearance will shine with optimism and self-assurance.

Once again, your subconscious thoughts, if harnessed properly, will help you achieve your goals.

Possible "Mind" Slogans:

"I will do it"

"I will win!"

"I think only optimistic thoughts"

"I love people"

"I am becoming more intelligent"

"I forgive some people and feel sorry for them"
"I feel good about life"
"I take full responsibility for my actions"
"I have peace of mind in every moment"

Write Your "Mind" Slogans:

_____

_____

_____

_____

_____

Let's now examine the third individual value: our work. Since we spend roughly a third of our lives working, why not find ways to enjoy our time at work? How can we create a positive and uplifting workplace mentality?

Start by identifying what is **good** at your workplace. Recall those desirable elements. Imagine the best parts of your job. Focus on viewing the less enjoyable parts as a learning experience, a source of motivation to seek a better life. If your work environment is not enjoyable, ask how you can improve your situation. Create ways to enhance your work life, apply your subconscious mind, and repeat the requested result with a strong sense of conviction.

Possible "Work" Slogans:

"I love my work"

"I highly enjoy my work"

"I like my employer and employees"

"I work hard and intense"

"I see only the positive aspect of work"

"I love what I do, and I do what I love"

Write Your "Work" Slogans:

_____

_____

_____

_____

_____

_____

_____

Remember, if you already score high with some values, you can always focus on the other values.

Even if you have low scores in some values, concentrate on improving what you best feel like doing. Sometimes, these efforts take time so feel free to alternate the order of your priorities. Be honest with yourself and take action!

Embracing positive changes is a key ingredient for pursuing happy life and making yourself a winner. If you rate yourself with low scores, don't obsess over your current weaknesses. Instead, immediately imagine improving each value. Through cognitive visualization, you shape your pathway to success. Visualizing future actions will help you attain and secure a well-balanced life.

For your money value, ask yourself, "How much money do I really want? How much do I need to achieve my life goals?" Regarding financial goals, avoid thinking about what other people may think because they may not share the same priorities and perspectives. Whether your financial goals are modest or not, do not let other people judge you. Since you earn the money, you should define your own level of success. Always remember, as important as money may seem, it still only represents **one** of eight values.

Possible "Money" Slogans:

"I will have $100,000 net worth by 20__"

"I will put $___ each month into my retirement account."

"I will earn $____ this year."

"I will pay off $___ debt this year."

"I will pay off my credit card."

"I will pay off my student loans."

Write Your "Money" Slogans:

_____

_____

_____

_____

_____

_____

Summary: The Four Individual Values

1) Body

2) Mind

3) Work

4) Money

In the novella, "The Happiest American" in Part II, you learned how you can reflect upon ideas as they come to you. Success happens when you fulfill your self-defined, visualized goals. Remember, as you encounter challenges in life, you can enable your pursuit for happiness by frequently referring to this handbook.

Fulfilling your four "individual" values will strengthen and prepare you to succeed in our four "relationship" goals. Strengthened people can then contribute greatly to their community and to one's country. A nation filled with goal-achieving optimistic citizens will shine as an example of hope for improving the world. By obtaining our individual goals, we enhance our abilities to love and serve others through our four "relationship" values.

Summary: The Four Relationship Values

1) **God**
2) **Country**
3) **Family**
4) **Friends**

First, examine your social status truthfully with these four "relationship" values. Then ask yourself, "How I can better myself in each area?"

Referring to your first value, **God,** how can you improve your relationship with God, or your spirituality? Only you can define and evaluate such a significant relationship.

There are many ways by which people practice or observe their spirituality.

Possible "Spiritual" Slogans:

"I thank God every day for what I have"

"I ask for guidance and strength from God"

"God is always a good God"

"With God, everything is possible"

"If God is with me, who can be against me"

"God, thank you for making my life precious"

"God, give me strength to be compassionate and loving"

Your *"Spiritual"* Slogans:

_____

_____

_____

_____

_____

_____

Our next relationship value is **"Country"** and your greater community. How would you define your current relationship and feelings towards your country and your community? Ask yourself what you can do for your country and community. Avoid thinking what the community owes you.

Possible "Country / Community" Slogans:

"I love my country."

I will do my best for my country."

"I will build a better future for all people."

"I help out in the community."

"Today, I will smile at people in my community."

"I do small things with great love for my country."

"I help others in need in the community."

Your "Country/Community" Slogans:

_____

_____

_____

_____

_____

_____

Remember, our forefathers sacrificed so much: we are so fortunate to enjoy life in a modern, wealthy democracy. Through appreciating our freedoms and pursuing justice, we can pursue our own happiness. Our successes and properties serve as a beacon of hope and optimism to the world.

Once you have decided how you can contribute to your country and your community, that has given you so much, continue onto our third "relationship" value: **family.**

How can you improve your family life? Each family has its own special needs and is unique by the composition of its members. How can you better appreciate your family? What grade would you give yourself for the **family** value? If you grade yourself low, think of how you can improve your family life.

Possible "Family" Slogans:
"I love my family and I support them 100%"

"I love my wife/husband'

"I love my kids"

"I encourage my family"

"I am patient with my family"

"I enjoy being with my family"

Your "Family" Slogans:

_____

_____

_____

_____

_____

The last "relationship" value includes your **friends**. First, what kinds of friends are in your life? We have four categories of friends: 1) *close* friends, 2) *good* friends, 3) *social* friends and 4) *false* friends. Embrace your close friends for these are the ones that remain with you through the worst of times. Most are "good" and "social" friends so we usually cannot expect these people to sacrifice much of their lives to help us. Beware of "false" friends who pretend to care about you but whenever hardships come along, they vanish.

How can you improve your relationships with your close, good, and social friends?

Again, define this on your own values. Create and use your slogans. For instance, repeat to yourself, "I have great friends." Soon, you will begin believing it and you will start cultivating great friendships. Your subconscious mind could yet do another service for you: it could help you to possibly convert some "false" friends into "good" ones.

Possible "Friends" Slogans:

"I realize I have close, good, social and false friends"

"I am fortunate to have great friends"

"I like and help my friends"

"Friendship builds bridges"

Write Your "Friends" Slogans:

_____

_____

_____

_____

_____

Now we have finished discussing all eight values: the four "individual" values (**body, mind, work, money**) and the four "relationship" values (**God, country, family, friends**).

You also have begun the important journey of honest self-evaluation. With this new focus, you will become aware that your life is being transformed and enriched by all eight values. You have undertaken to walk the pathway of happiness.

Again, realize how fortunate you are to be alive!

It is a miracle that you can take advantage of this time to benefit from this book – by living in such a free country, with so many possibilities and opportunities before you. Success is a consequential achievement of a balanced, happy life that has been created not by chance, but by the force of your willpower, commitment and imagination. The road to happiness is paved by positive messages that visualize each step of your life's journey.

The Eight Words

Understanding these eight words will help you obtain what you most desire. Optimism is fueled by focus and determination. Maintaining a positive attitude towards others naturally creates opportunities and possibilities because people are generally drawn towards positive rather than critical or negative thinking. People crave and want happiness. You can spread those feelings while enabling your chances for success.

Remember: always write down your goals. Make a mental commitment, with a realistic timeframe.

My Major Goal is:

_____

_____

_____

My next most important Goal is:

_____

_____

_____

Then, start repeating your desired **goal,** imagining that you have already accomplished it.

Remember the power of a self-fulfilling prophecy: do not "curse" yourself with thoughts of failure. Speaking your ideas and goals out loud, on a regular basis, will turn your ideas into reality.

Yes, you **can** create your reality and your future by choosing and using the right kinds of words to organize and run your life.

Also, by frequently **repeating** your **goals** to yourself, you will discover that repetition boosts, supports and re-enforces your emotional commitment to completing your goals. The key is to cast aside your doubts and **do it.**

Do it now!

Repetition works because it channels your mental energies, while filtering out distractions. Ritualize your repetition during key parts of the day such as when you go to sleep or wake up.

Each day, write down your eight most important tasks. Over time, repetition solidifies your personalized goals within your extremely powerful sub-conscious mind.

It is essential to make sure your tasks and slogans not only directly relate to your goal, but that you **prioritize** them.

185

By doing so, you will invest your energies on more efficiently obtaining the results you seek, while also reducing procrastination or unnecessary work on what you know to be minor, unrelated tasks.

For the best results, reserve some quality time to **think and learn**. Each morning, or at the time you know you'e at your mental peak for the day, set aside some "thinking time." Write down ideas that come to you when you **think.**

Think of ways to increase your service to your customers, colleagues, friends, family and community. The magic of **think** is found in its inherent creativity. Thoughts form into words. Words prod one into action. Actions net results.

Service, or **serving**, is natural for most people because most people don't live in isolation: they cooperate with each other and depend on each other. As you share your successes and resources with your family, friends, and community, you will enrich and enhance a greater sense not only your life, and give it more meaning, but you will exert the same effect on those around you.

By sharing the goodness in your life with others, you will create even more opportunities for future successes.

Above all, be **honest** with yourself and others. Take responsibility for your actions, no matter how painful.

Encourage others, especially those involved in making your goals come true, to act the same. Express your true self. You can do that by communicating what you **really think.**

Exercising **honesty** is the most powerful act you can make in a world full of deception and distrust. It is a powerful instrument for good that will align your personal relationships with your personal thoughts. If you do not cherish and honor the words you give to others, you risk disharmonizing and squandering important relationships and opportunities.

Last, but not least, cultivate a *grateful heart.* Choose to be grateful, every chance you can. Make a habit of thanking God, for "Every good thing comes from God." So give thanks! Express gratitude for what you have and what you may receive. You **know** that you can – and **will** -- eventually **become** what you **think.** about most.

So be careful with what you **think and say; encourage yourself** by **thinking** only positive, uplifting thoughts. Brush aside and ignore negative thoughts that suddenly enter your mind; throw them into a mental waste basket.

The thoughts generated by your own *gratitude* create the link between yourself and the Creator of all there is. If you recognize your life desires with a sense of *gratitude*, you can fully access your own creative power. Achievements are often obtained by influencing the subconscious mind in beneficial ways. For example, athletes often adopt a positive mental attitude and combine that with their goals. They often unintentionally program their sub-conscious minds to work for them.

Create Positive Mental Images of Your Goals and Life

Select an image. Record it in your sub-conscious mind. By fixating your conscious mind with an intense purpose, your selected mental images will communicate with your sub-conscious mind. Repetition links both minds.

The Results

Next, begin watching for, and expecting, tangible, physical manifestations that will result in the actual realization of your mental goals. Seek to identify each step of your progress as you form and then exercise faith and the keys to success that you have been given. Do it with intensity, **realizing that it is already a reality.** With repetition, belief and faith, you will get to where you want to be.

The result: your chief aims in life **will be fulfilled.** Because of your commitment to your highest goals, having chosen to persevere, to deal honestly, and to use these keys to create your own future, you will find true happiness. Through your willpower, imagination and focus, the good in your life will grow, overwhelming every defeat with real, tangible accomplishments. Get ready for miracles! And as they arrive, enriching your life, and the lives of others, you will realize your greatest potentials, maximize your happiest, experience tremendous success.

PART IV:
CONCLUSION

Now, you have choices to make. Goals to set.

Repeat to yourself: ***"Dreams come true by identifying my goals and matching them with my values."***

Life is a journey about **you** and **your** ambitions.

Reflect and continue thinking about what you just read. Commit yourself to learn and to grow by setting positive, personal goals. Know that many positive goals bring desirable consequences. Your incredible subconscious mind can help you redirect your life in the direction you choose. If you focus on prioritizing your goals and if you apply the principles described in this book, you will obtain a successful, balanced happy life with peace of mind.

You can do almost anything you want in life as long as you believe it and not purposely harm others. Once you use these principles, your world will become better. If you utilize your resources in positive ways, you will make this planet better for everyone.

<u>You live on this planet for four reasons to:</u>

(1) love, (2) serve, (3) create, and (4) enjoy.

When you apply these four reasons and our chosen slogans to your eight values and when you apply those with the eight words, you obtain a complete happiness.

Now you have a choice. You can continue living your life as before, or you can change your life by applying the methods in this book. Tell yourself to act now. I urge you to make the right choice. You have come a long way in this path of self-discovery. If you ardently desire a goal and sincerely believe and enthusiastically act upon it, you will achieve results. Now, you have almost finished the first goal of success -- reading this book! Congratulate yourself. **You have been given the keys to become all that you want to be.**

Use this book to stay focused on what is important for you and your relationships with **God, community, family, friends, body, mind, work, and money.**

If you use this knowledge wisely and study its principles, your life will change for the better, in ways you formerly could only imagine. Yet it is through using your imagination and wedding it to your willpower and intelligence, that what once were just dreams become goals, and goals become real events.

You **can** create your future! You **can** make your goals become real!

Reflect upon these facts. Make these positive messages a central part of your life.

Carry your slogans with you, wherever you go. After all, by doing this for **you**, your life can change for the benefit of all humankind.

190

So now you know the secrets. You now can choose to **live** the positive slogans. Share these with your friends.

Take advantage of this simple message, and let's make the world better, together!

Be an optimist. Choose the positive, and become the captain of your destiny. Set your own standards of success. Take command of your future, and make it real.

Congratulate yourself, knowing that you have already embarked upon the pathway of success ... and the world will benefit from it.

Refer to this book many times: don't let your chances for success and happiness slip away from you again!

This book will help you stay on track as you continue your journey. When you reflect and **act upon** the messages in this little book, you will realize true success. Set your goals for the eight values: **body, mind, work, money, God, country, family and friends.** Most people feel helpless about changing their lives for the better, because they don't believe in themselves. But now is the time to start believing. You're alive! You have power to kick your bad habits aside, one by one, and to take up the better ones, one by one. Follow the pathway you've been shown, and the forecast is bright. Believe you have already succeeded, and you will succeed! Be an optimist, my friend, and watch the miracles happen!

A NEW BEGINNING!

About Ulf Sandström

In 1978 Ulf Sandström, Esq., started studying the important questions of 'Why are we here?' 'What is the meaning of life? What can our sub-conscious mind do to us? How can we become more optimistic?' After finishing Law School at the prestigious Uppsala University, Sandström practiced law in Sweden before he and his family emigrated to the United States. His book, Du Blir Vad Du Tänker (published 1986) was in print for over 20 years, selling over 200,000 copies in Scandinavia.

In 1986, Ulf used his technique of the progressive realization of the eight worthy ideals, as described in this book, to make a profitable and successful move to the United States with his wife, Annika, and their two sons. In America, they owned and operated the chic, upscale women's boutique, Olivia, at fashionable St. Armand's Circle in Sarasota, Florida.

In 1988, Sandström created the Sweden Club of Sarasota. For many years, he helped expand and manage the club. He was a longtime member of the International Rotary Club and Toastmasters. He also was involved in wholesale import and export businesses. In 2000, he and his family became proud American citizens.

About Josiah R. Baker

Josiah R. Baker, Ph.D., is a tenured Economics and Finance Professor at Methodist University in North Carolina. His research focuses on public policies. In 2004, he was a Fulbright Scholar in Bolivia. He has authored five textbooks, nine novels, two academic books and a poetry book. He also has contributed to eight other textbooks, two encyclopedias, and published numerous articles in major newspapers and magazines.

Dr. Baker regularly travels throughout the world for his research and has spent substantial amounts of time in Japan, Russia, the Netherlands, Norway, and Sweden.

While Dr. Baker has taught hundreds of courses in economics, political science and geography, prior to his academic career, he worked as a journalist in the U.S. and in Europe.

His book is *Religion, Politics, and Polarization: How Religiopolitical Conflict is Changing Congress and American Democracy,* which won the 2015 Morris Rosenberg Award for outstanding research in Sociology from the Washington DC Sociological Society.

Bibliography:

Allen, James. *As a Man Thinketh*.

Anthony, Robert. *Think Big*.

Aurelius, Marcus. *Meditations*.

Baker, Josiah R. *Cuts of the Mind*.

Bettger, Frank. *How I Raised Myself from Failure to Success in Selling The Bible*.

Binstock, Louis. *The Power of Maturity*.

Blanchard, Ken, Hybels, Bill, and Phil Hodges. *Leadership by the Book*.

Bristol, Claude M. *The Magic of Believing*.

Buscaglia, Leo. LOVE.

Buzan, Tony. *Make the Most of Your Mind*.

Canfield, Jack & Mark Victor Hansen. *Chicken Soup for The Soul*.

Carlson, Richard. *Don't Sweat the Small Stuff*.

Carnegie, Dale. *How to Win Friends and Influence People*.

Chopra, Deepak. *The Seven Spiritual Laws of Success*.

Cialdini, Dr. Robert. *Influence. The Psychology of Persuasion*.

Clason, George S. *The Richest Man in Babylon*.

Collins, Gary R. *The Magnificent Mind*.

Confucius. *Analects*.

Conwell, Russell H., *Acres of Diamonds*.

Coue', Emile. *Self-Mastery through Conscious Autosuggestion*.

Cousin, Norman. *Anatomy of an Illness Perceived by a Patient*.

Cousin, Norman. *Headfirst: the Biology of Hope*.

Covey, Stephen R. *The 7 Habits of Highly Effective People*.

Dalai Lama & Howard C. Cutler. *The Art of Happiness*.

Davidson, Richard. *Visions of Compassion*.

De Bono, Edward. *The Use of Lateral Thinking. The Declaration of Independence*.

Doman, Glenn & Janet. *How To Multiply Your Baby's Intelligence*.

Dyer, Wayne W. *Your Erroneous Zones*.

Dyer, Wayne W. *There is a Spiritual Solution to Every Problem.*

Dyer, Wayne W. *You'll See It When You Believe It.*

Emerson, Ralph Waldo. *Compensation.*

Emerson, Ralph Waldo. *Experience.*

Fox, Emmet. *The Sermon of the Mount.*

Frankl, Victor. *Man's Search for Meaning. The Autobiography of Benjamin Franklin.*

Garfield, Jane. *Creative Dreaming.*

Garfield, Jane. *Healing Power of Dreams.*

Gawain, Shakti. *Creative Visualization.*

Getty, J. Paul. *How to Be Rich.*

Goleman, Daniel. *Emotional Intelligence.*

Harris, Thomas A. *I'm Ok-You're Ok.*

Hernacki, Mike. *The Ultimate Secret to Getting Absolutely Everything You Want.*

Hill, Napoleon. *The Law of Success.*

Hill, Napoleon. *Think and Grow Rich.*

Hill, Napoleon. *Grow Rich! With Peace of Mind.*

https://www.lonelyplanet.com/usa/hawaii/background/history/a/nar/04a2b187-1bf4-409c-8474-2d0031d67eba/361972

Hubbard, Elbert. *A Message to Garcia.*

Johnson, Wendell. *People in Quandaries.*

Keyes Jr., Ken. *Handbook to Higher Consciousness.*

Michael Le Boeuf. *Working Smart.*

Maxwell Maltz. *Psycho-Cybernetics & Self-Fulfillment.*

Mandino, Og. *The Greatest Salesman in the World.*

McGraw, Philip C. *Self Matters.*

McWilliams, Peter. *You Can't Afford the Luxury of a Negative Thought.*

Moody, Raymond A. *Life After Life.*

Moody, Raymond A. *Laugh After Laugh: The Healing Power of Humor.*

Murphy, Joseph. *The Power of Your Subconscious Mind.*

Murphy, Joseph. *The Infinite Power to be Rich.*

Nightingale, Earl. *The Strangest Secret.*

Ogilvie, Lloyd John. *Conversation with God.*

Peale, Norman Vincent. *Enthusiasm Makes the Difference.*

Peale, Norman Vincent. *The Power of Positive Thinking*.

Peale, Norman Vincent. *The True Joy of Positive Living*.

Peale, Norman Vincent. *Thought Conditioner*.

Peck, M. Scott. *The Road Less Traveled*.

Perl, Sheri. *Healing from the Inside Out*.

Redfield, James. *The Celestine Prophecy*.

Robbins, Anthony. *Awakening the Giant Within*.

Roger, John and Peter McWilliams. *You Can't Afford A Negative Thought*.

Russell, Bertrand. *The Conquest of Happiness*.

Schwartz, David J. *The Magic of Thinking Big*.

Schuller, Robert. *Tough Times Never Last But Tough People Do*.

Seligman, Martin E. P. *Learned Optimism*.

Siegel, Bernie. *Love, Medicine, and Miracles*.

Simonton, Carl. *Getting Well Again*.

Smiles, Samuel. *Self-Help*.

Stone, W. Clement. *The Success System that Never Fail*.

Stone, W. Clement and Napoleon Hill. *Success through a Positive Mental Attitude*.

Swindell, Charles R. *Growing Strong in the Seasons of Life*.

Thoreau, Henry David. *Walden*.

Tracy, Brian. *Maximum Achievement*.

The United States Constitution.

The Napoleon Hill Foundation, *Napoleon Hill's Keys to Success, the 17 Principles of Personal Achievement*.

Waitley, Denis. *The Psychology of Winning*.

Ward, Bernie. *Think Yourself WELL*.

Wattles, Wallace D. *The Science of Getting Rich*.

Weiss, Brian. *Many Lives, Many Masters*.

Weiss, Brian. *Through Time into Healing*.

Zahourek, Rothly. *Relaxation and Imagery*.

Zigler, Zig. *See You at the Top*

Zilbergeld, Bernie and Arnold Lazarus. *Mind Power: GettingWhat You Want through Mental Training*.

In Memorandum...Sandström, Ulf T.

Mar. 8, 1952 – Oct. 1, 2020

Ulf Teddy Sandström (born March 8, 1952, Stockholm, Sweden), a Swedish-American best-selling author, entrepreneur, retail executive, and philanthropist died in Sarasota, Florida, on October 1, 2020. Ulf passionately practiced and promoted the power of positive thinking throughout his adult life. As an avid reader and philosopher, he read many hundreds of books.

Raised by his military academy professor father, Colonel Sture Sandström, and his mother Alli, a beauty queen and socialite, Ulf grew up in different parts of Sweden, but especially loved life in Karlsberg Palace in Stockholm. During his teen years in northernmost Sweden, Ulf was an accomplished youth chess champion and believed by many to be Norbotten county's best soccer player. As a student he earned top grades in mathematics and in the sciences. Upon finishing high school, in 1971-72, Ulf served in the Swedish Navy. After training at the Muskö naval base, Sandström served on Sweden's last frigate-class vessel where he first explored the world, sailing across the Atlantic, Pacific, and Indian Oceans. After completing his military service, Ulf continued his journeys by working for the Gripsholms world cruise line. For two years, 1972-1973, the cruise line took Ulf along the coasts of Latin America, the Caribbean islands, Africa, India, Asia, but most importantly, America. When his ship first approached the American shores near New York City, Ulf heard their intercom system tune into a local New York radio station. While listening to popular American rock songs in English, Ulf got his first glance of the Statue of Liberty and lower Manhattan and instantly decided, "This is where I must live!"

With America, it was love at first sight. From that point onward, Ulf planned, plotted, and calculated how he could make his American dream happen. After saving enough funds from working on the cruise line, with considerable encouragement from his father, Ulf gained admission and studied law at Uppsala University, Scandinavia's most prestigious law school. Located just north of Stockholm, Ulf pursued his passions in philosophy and politics. In 1976, Ulf met the love of his life, Annika Hallström. On that first night that they met, Ulf made a seemingly outrageous offer to take Annika to America. From that day onward, the two became inseparable, engaged, and married after Sandström completed law school in 1978.

After honeymooning in California, the young couple relocated to southwestern Sweden in Halmstad where Annika established her first clothing boutique, *Olivia*, and Ulf created his law firm, *Hallands Juristfirma*. While he and his wife built their respective businesses, Ulf became more deeply involved in reading motivational materials, including the works of Dale Carnegie, Norman Vincent Peale, and Napoleon Hill. Always active in community affairs, Sandström joined Halmstad's City Club and became the President of *Hallands Merchant Association*, 1985-1986. However, his American dream never diminished.

The year 1986 proved to be Ulf's most pivotal year. His years of research resulted in publishing his first book "You Become What You Think" (*"Du Blir Vad Du Tänker"*), co-authored with Yngve Borgström. Particularly popular with Middle School educators and counseling centers, it endured as a best-seller in Sweden and Norway for over twenty years. Later, with Borgström, he published another book "You Become What You Dream Of" (*"Du Blir Vad Du Drömmer Om"*). Prompted by the success of his book sales, Sandström finally realized his dream by moving to the tropical paradise of Sarasota, Florida.

Arriving on July 17, 1986, (a date which is enshrined on a plaque in his house) with his wife and two young sons, but without a job or a residency permit, Ulf instantly fell in love with Saint Armand's Circle and felt determined to establish his commercial operations there. Despite some initial setbacks, including cultural adjustments, by 1992 the Sandströms' second *Olivia* far exceeded the successes of the original. Next, Sandström launched other businesses, including Saint Armand's Dry Cleaning and Sweden Trade (an import-export and publishing firm), which eventually imported Stockholm Beer.

As Sandström had in Sweden, he immersed himself into community service which included membership of the Rotary Club of Sarasota Keys, the Rotary Club of Saint Armand Circle, the International Platform Association, and Toastmasters of Sarasota. In 1988, Ulf sought to bring together the region's Swedish immigrant community by creating the Swedish Club of Sarasota. The club expanded from a small, singular social event among a few friends to many hundreds of members. Activities included an annual Lucia Celebration held at the St. Armand's Circle Key Lutheran Church in December, pea soup parties, shrimp feasts, crayfish Swedish style, and socializing on Florida's beautiful gulf coast. Aside from founding the Sweden club, on numerous occasions, he served as its president.

A few years after finally obtaining his citizenship, in 2003, Ulf resumed his writing career by finishing his first work in English, "*The Road to Happiness.*" Two years later, a fourth book, "*The Magic Silver Coin*" was published. For the remainder of Sandström's life, he gave motivational talks promoting the messages of his books. Shortly before Ulf's death, he completed his long-awaited magnum opus, "The Optimist", a compilation of stories and his life's research involving the power of positive thinking. Aside from celebrating over thirty years of success for his Florida-based businesses, Ulf relentlessly motivated and encouraged his sons' entrepreneurial efforts. Ulf is remembered as a man who deeply loved his family, loved the American dream, was always kind and generous to his many friends, and left a positive impression wherever he went.